Simon Newcomb

A Critical Examination of Our Financial Policy During the Southern Rebellion

Simon Newcomb

A Critical Examination of Our Financial Policy During the Southern Rebellion

ISBN/EAN: 9783337000189

Printed in Europe, USA, Canada, Australia, Japan

Cover: Foto ©Suzi / pixelio.de

More available books at **www.hansebooks.com**

A CRITICAL EXAMINATION

OF OUR

FINANCIAL POLICY

DURING THE

SOUTHERN REBELLION.

BY

SIMON NEWCOMB.

NEW YORK:
D. APPLETON AND COMPANY,
443 & 445 BROADWAY.
1865.

ENTERED according to Act of Congress, in the year 1865, by
D. APPLETON & COMPANY,
In the Clerk's Office of the District Court of the United States for the Southern District of New York.

PREFACE.

The objects of the following essay are to trace our present financial system to its effects on the power of our Government, the permanence of our institutions, the future well-being of society, and other great national interests; to show how certain principles of social science are illustrated in its workings; and, incidentally, to inquire in what ways it may be improved. The work generally avoids those topics of merely passing importance, the discussion of which belongs to the daily press, and confines itself to questions of permanent interest. Aiming its criticisms at the root of evil rather than its branches, its fundamental doctrines are few and simple.

The great desire of the author has been to produce full conviction of the truth of these doctrines. He has, therefore, sought to found them solely on those facts of human nature which, established by the general experience of mankind, must be admitted by all unprejudiced men, and those facts of history which are absolutely indisputable. For the same reason he has avoided that large class of questions which do not admit of a decided answer.

The first two chapters were suggested by the general disposition manifested in our legislative halls and our organs of public opinion, to ignore all that the nineteenth contury has done for financial science, and to adhere entirely to the views and practices of the eighteenth. Their object is therefore less to develop a complete system of ideas than to amend the most serious defects in the popular Political Economy.

CONTENTS.

CHAPTER I.

MONEY AND TRADE, ... 9

The Laws of Trade Founded on Human Nature—Object of a Government Financial System—Popular Errors respecting Finance—The Laws of Value—Popular Theories respecting the Degradation of our Standard—Speculation—The Money Market; what Controls it?

CHAPTER II.

THE FINANCIAL ELEMENTS OF MILITARY STRENGTH, 34

The Measure of Military Strength—Money not a Source of Power—Frugality the real element of Power—Political Economy not Conserved with our Highest Good—Should we Save our Gold?—Our War Expenditure, what does it Mean?

CHAPTER III.

OUR DEBT AND OUR TAXES, ... 60

    Relation of the Individual to the State—Supposed Benefits of the British Debt—Perils in which our Debt will Involve us—How to Carry on War without Borrowing—When Advisable to Borrow—Ought our Debt to be Taxable?

CHAPTER IV.

THE LEGAL TENDER NOTES—THEIR EFFECT ON PUBLIC CREDIT, ... 88

    What the Legal Tender Act was—Failure to give the Notes any Element of Value—The Evil, one of Principle—Payment of the Principal of the Public Debt—The Price of Gold and Government Bonds—Causes of the Depreciation in the Gold Value of the Bonds—How all future Loans should be Contracted.

CHAPTER V.

INFLUENCE OF THE LEGAL TENDER NOTES ON PRIVATE FAITH AND THE BUSINESS OF THE COUNTRY, ... 122

    Laws of Value of the Currency—Effects of Depreciation on Banks, etc.,—Effects of Depreciation on Ownership of Property—Effects of Depreciation on our Future Welfare.

CHAPTER VI.

NECESSITY OF PAPER MONEY—THE LESSONS OF HISTORY. 146

    Popular Views—The English Bank Money—Continental Money, what it did—Rise and Fall of Assignats.

CHAPTER VII.

WERE LEGAL TENDER NOTES NECESSARY? . . 159

The True Functions of Notes—Our Financial History had Specie Payments been maintained—Ought the Notes to be Irredeemable?—Ought they to have been Legal Tender for Principal of the Public Debt?—Was it necessary that they should be a Legal Tender for Private Debts?—Examination of Arguments for the Legal Tender Clause—Causes of our Financial Mistakes.

CHAPTER VIII.

THE NATIONAL BANKING SYSTEM, ... 199

Functions of Banks—Popular Errors respecting our Currency—Who Lends to the Government?—Working of our National Banking System—Unwise Restrictions in the way on which they might use their Votes—Their Functions as Fiscal Agents.

A CRITICAL EXAMINATION

OF OUR FINANCIAL POLICY.

CHAPTER I

MONEY AND TRADE.

The feelings and opinions, the hopes and fears of the million, form an ocean of thought in which the individual is lost as the drop is lost in the Atlantic. Tempests of passion agitate the surface of this ocean, but they cannot change its general level, nor drive it from its set bounds. It ebbs and flows under the influence of victory and defeat, and a thousand other causes, many of which we can trace only in their effects. Like the Atlantic, this ocean is at once the most uncontrollable of powers, and the most manageable of instruments. Address the sea; reason with it; legislate against its tides; quarrel with its storms; enact that it shall change its winds; complain of its destructiveness; demonstrate to it that there is no good cause for the fury of its waves, and you are impotent. Accept it, with all its vagaries, as unchangeable facts; study its winds and currents as they are, without seeking to change them; trim your sails and guide your helm accordingly, and you are carried in safety to your desired harbor. With all the improvements man has made in navigation since the time the Phœnician first launched his boat on the Mediterranean, he has never brought a breath of wind under his control, or commanded a single billow. Yet the most adverse wind is his servant, and takes him whither he will. In a similar way kings and statesmen have swayed "the rod of empire" over millions, and made the very selfishness of mankind to minister to them without causing any change in human nature, or altering the motives of a single individual.

Of this mass of thought and opinion none is more intractable when we seek to control it, none more manageable when we adopt the proper means to use it, than that which relates to money, prices, and credit. No sooner do men begin to trade in great numbers than they find laws of trade which are beyond individual control. They find that an increased supply of an article will diminish its price, and an increased demand raise it; that goods will flow to the best market in defiance of every thing except forcible prevention; that the man who sells cheapest will have most custom, though hated by the community. So long as no attempt is made to interfere with the orderly operation of these laws they might pass with little notice. But, by and by the king, or the Government, finds that they are operating so as to be detrimental to his interests; that the prices of articles which he wishes to obtain, articles which suddenly become indispensable to the public good, jump up with equal suddenness, that his promises to pay are not properly appreciated by the community; that men will prefer the money which he cannot obtain to that which he has to pay with. He attributes all this to the machinations of his enemies, and the heartless selfishness of individuals, and forthwith resorts to penal and mandatory legislation for a remedy. He enacts that his promises to pay shall be as valuable as gold. Gold instantly disappears. He then enacts that they shall be legal tender. Immediately every man who has goods for sale doubles or trebles their prices, so that the Government is still no better off than before. As a last resort he enacts that bread and meat shall be sold at old prices. Bread and meat thereupon disappear like the gold, except as they are sold clandestinely at the increased prices. The butchers no longer come to market, the bakers disappear from the community like icebergs melt in the Gulf Stream. The farmers cease to cultivate their fields, engines stop working, mines fill up, grass grows in the streets, starvation and ruin stare the public in the face.

Experiments like this have been tried by kings and princes and legislators from time immemorial, and always with the same result. The weakest Government, and the most powerful; the king and the president, the despotism and the republic; the ferocity of the triumvirate and the wisdom of Parliament have been alike impotent. Why is this? Why cannot two men or two millions of men, acting through their chosen representatives, mutually agree that they will furnish the products of their labor in certain quantities and on certain fixed terms? What laws regulate the value of gold, the price of government stocks, and the price of goods? These questions must have risen in the philosophical mind on every exhibition of the phenomena to which we have alluded. In answering them a new science was constructed, that of Political Economy.

This science showed how the selfishness of individuals was made, in the social system, to contribute in the highest degree to the public good. It showed that men labored primarily, not for the benefit of others, but of themselves; that they benefited others by their labor on condition that others should benefit them; that they would dispose of their labor in such manner and give its products to such persons as to receive the greatest possible benefit in return; and that thus, while every man would really be working from pure selfishness, that very motive would lead him to exert himself so as to do the greatest good to the community.

It has also shown that the function of money is simply to cause these exchanges to be made in the way most advantageous to all parties; so that every man shall be able to receive whatever article he most wishes in exchange for his goods, no matter whether the man who makes this article shall want his goods or not; that the value of this money, if useless for other purposes than money, is fixed entirely by the wants of the community; and that the value of all manufactured goods, and indeed of every thing else, is in the long run measured by the amount of labor necessary to their production, or their possession.

It can also be shown that for a people to fix among themselves and mutually a standard of prices, such that every man will have to exchange his goods for so little money that he would in his own heart rather have the goods than the money, is simply to introduce a system of communism, in which men will have to work, not for what they receive in exchange for their goods, but for the benefit of the commonwealth. True, if men were neither indolent nor selfish the community would then enjoy nearly as much wealth as they actually do; but the fact is that men always have been indolent and selfish, and always will be. These characteristics are not to be deplored; they only keep in operation the just principle that the fruits of every man's toil belong to himself, and that he has the right to fix the terms on which he will part with them.

Political economy as a pure science is founded on this postulate of human nature: that every man will dispose of his labor in such a way as to promote to the greatest possible extent the objects of his desire; and will endeavor to attain any definite end with the least possible amount of irksome labor. The savage and the sage alike exhibit this characteristic, they differ only in the nature of their desires. On it is founded the science of Political Economy. All the conclusions of this science are perfectly true and quite applicable to practice so far as the actions of men are governed by it, and no longer. Now, it is a fact of observation which has held true in all ages and countries, that all voluntary exchanges of property between man and man are made in obedience to the above postulate. No man parts with his goods except he is to receive in exchange something which he prefers to them. No man will work two days, or give two dollars for an object of desire, when he can get it for one. Any government polity which supposes men, in managing their money matters, to be actuated by benevolence, malevolence, public spirit, political enmity, or any other motive than self-interest, is fundamentally defective, and will be sure to fail. Hence, to answer the question, "What will a man do with his money?" it is only necessary to discover what it is for his interest to do.

We are not at present concerned with the whole of this science, but with an application of its principles to our financial policy during the present war. Four years ago our Government was attacked and our liberties threatened by a combination at once the most malignant and the most unscrupulous which any people ever had to contend against. The Government and the social system which we were to transmit to our posterity had to be decided by the issues of battle. A vast amount of work had to be done in the way of feeding and clothing armies, casting cannon, shot, and shell, and putting in operation all the complicated enginery of modern warfare. The war once inevitable, each of our twenty millions of people was willing to bear his share of its burden, rather than see his country subjected to those who would conquer it. To distribute this burden so that none should be able to shirk his just share, or throw it upon his neighbor; so that the total burden should be as light as possible; so that the ownership of property should be disturbed, the business and growth of the country impeded, and honesty and frugality discouraged as little as possible; this was or ought to have been the financial problem. True, it was disguised under the form of raising loans and levying taxes, so that the end really aimed at was almost lost sight of, and to this circumstance all the mistakes that were made may perhaps be traced.

The attention of the reader is called to the means employed to attain these ends. It is proposed to examine how far the burden of the war has been equitably distributed, and what effect the policy pursued has had and is likely to have upon public credit, private honesty, and the ownership of property. The whole foundation of our reasoning shall be admitted principles or indisputable facts, and all appeal to or respect for mere authority shall be avoided.

It will conduce to clearness if we first try to form a definite idea of what financial science really is. Notwithstanding the simplicity of its principles, and their continued illustration in the affairs of life, the most crude and impractical ideas are entertained respecting them. We are prone to fall into two great errors, closely connected with each other: firstly, that there is no such thing as financial science; and secondly, that questions of finance are too mysterious to be comprehended by the people at large.

The speculations of many of our newspapers and other organs of public opinion illustrate the first mistake. Their reasonings on questions of government credit are remarkably like the speculations of the ancient philosophers on questions of natural philosophy. We find the same disposition to frame imaginative theories, and the same indisposition to learn any thing from experience. We see every effect, every fall in stocks, and every rise in gold attributed to some cause, but how the cause produces the effect is left as much a mystery as how a comet or an eclipse used to cause the death of a king or the fall of an empire. The money market is peopled with good and evil spirits, with "gorgons, hydras, and chimeras dire," who are waging a perpetual war, or playing an endless game of Stygian ten-pins, using government stocks for the pins. Like those household spirits who are always ready to masticate a child without reference to the calls of their stomachs, or the gustatory pleasure to be derived from the operation, these bulls and bears, hobgoblins of the stock market, are not animated by any well-defined motives except a Satanic desire to destroy the government credit. It can, I trust, be shown to the satisfaction of every thinking man, that all these sprites, including that king of hobgoblins the gold speculator, are as powerless to injure the government credit as they are to change the course of the wind.

The second error to which we have referred is worthy of much more careful examination. That the principles of finance, like the art of banking, are to be learned by long experience behind a counter, and that those only who have had this experience are qualified to judge of the effects of financial measures, is an opinion so respectable and conservative that it may seem an art of presumption to controvert it. There is a disposition to look on finance as an art to be learned in school or the counting-house, rather than a science to be studied by the aid of human nature, and the use of sound logic. In opposition to this view it is maintained that common sense, close study, and attentive thought, with such experiential knowledge as every one may derive from the observation of current events are all that is necessary to enable any one to comprehend the working and the effects of any financial system, and to judge the arguments for and against it; and that a lawyer may therefore be as good a judge of such a system as a banker, provided that he will make himself master of the principles on which it is founded.

It will be universally admitted that experience can increase any man's power of correctly judging the effects of a new measure only when the things to be judged are similar to those which he has met with in experience. For instance, if a banker had always done business in a community which would allow nothing but coin to circulate as money, he would not thereby be better qualified to judge of the finances of a people whose circulating medium was irredeemable paper. Nay, he would be rather worse qualified, because he would be likely to adopt conclusions founded on his former experience, without duly considering the change of circumstances; he might consider money as being simply money, whatever its material, and totally forget that paper and metallic money are governed by entirely different laws. To judge the effects of a new measure adapted to new circumstances, requires experience of old measures much less than sound judgment, a clear comprehension of human nature, and a clear understanding of Political Economy.

But if we propose to put an old plan once more in operation, will not the advice of those who have seen the old plan work be of great value? Undoubtedly it will. A young cashier of a new bank will seldom fail to be benefited by the advice of an old cashier. The advice of Washington, Franklin, and Hamilton, who saw the rise, fall, and effects of the Continental money, would have been invaluable when it was first proposed to issue greenbacks. Still more valuable would have been the advice of Mr. John Stuart Mill, because he not only knew what had been the paper-money experience of past generations, but in addition thoroughly understood the principles which must underlie every financial system. His opinion ought therefore to have been entitled to more weight than that of any banker or board of trade.

The weight which any opinion ought to carry with it depends very much on the reasons assigned for it. In a science so exact as that of political economy, we can trace the effect of every intelligible cause. If, then, we are informed, on authority, that such a measure will produce evil effects, and such another measure good effects, we may reasonably demand to know *how* this good or evil is to be produced. If the authority fails to explain to our entire satisfaction the relation between the cause and the effect which he predicts, if he claims that it is something which no one but financiers can understand, then we may safely reject his advice. It is not enough that we know certain effects, good or evil, to have followed certain measures; we must also be able to understand the machinery by which these effects were produced. It is now proposed to elucidate some of the most elementary principles which govern the working of every system of financial machinery.

In the first place, the *desires* and *opinions* of men are to be accepted as fundamental facts, without criticizing the foundation on which they rest. Government credit is a fact, not a mathemetical theorem. It is not to be measured by calculating our resources, praising our honesty, and demonstrating our ability to pay, but by observing what our bonds sell for in the public market. To say that men ought to give more or less than they do, because the bonds are really worth more or less, is as idle as to say that stones ought to float, or wood sink. The financier is not concerned with what ought to be, but with what is; not with what men ought to think, but with what they do think. He does not seek to mould public opinion, for he knows that the money market is insensible to argument or expostulation. Men are determined to be their own judges of what is for their own pecuniary interests. We have had pamphlets proving that we are amply able to pay off our national debt, and publications trying to show that such payment is impossible; but the price of government bonds refused to respond to either argument. During the winter of 1862–'3 the value of 20 year six per cent. bonds gradually fell far below that of legal tender notes. During the fall the public was almost daily lectured on the absurdity of preferring a debt which bore no interest, and which depreciated twenty or thirty per cent. below coin, to a debt which bore interest in coin, but the lecturers might as well have talked to the winds. The bonds continued to fall until, with the improvement in the military situation, and the increased issue of notes, the money market slackened, and the demand for the bonds began, from this cause, to increase. Deeds, not words, is emphatically the maxim of the stock market.

In the next place the fundamental postulate of political economy already alluded to, that every man will seek to attain the objects of his desire at the smallest expense of labor, is to be taken for granted, else financial science can have no existence. Actions not in accordance with this principle are mere child's play.* Our whole monetary and industrial fabric rests upon it. From it follow the laws of value, and price, which we shall briefly set forth and illustrate.

1. The real value of an article, money included, is measured by the least amount of labor necessary to its possession. If a barrel of flour costs three days' labor, and a coat costs twelve, then one coat will, on the average, sell for as much as four barrels of flour. So long as an ounce of gold can be got as

---

* When Vanderbilts arise in sufficient number to give us an iron-clad navy, it will be time to cite examples of patriotic munificence as exceptions to this rule.

easily as a coat can be made, we may be sure that the latter will sell for as much as the former.

2. The relative value of articles, thus fixed, fluctuates under the influence of variations in the supply and demand. But the equilibrium cannot be permanently changed by the action of these causes, because, if they continue, men will gradually give up the production of those articles which are too cheap, and apply themselves to those which are too dear, until, by competition, the equilibrium of prices is restored. Indeed, a largely-increased demand, if permanent, will generally diminish the value of the article, because things can be made cheaper when made in large quantities.

3. Whenever the business of a country rises above mere barter, a common accepted standard, by which every man can estimate the value of his goods, becomes indispensable. A designated weight of one of the precious metals forms the best standard attainable, because these metals are universally desired, and subject to no serious fluctuations of value. Hence they have been used for this purpose from the earliest ages. The *price* of an article is its value, measured by the accepted standard. By a change in the standard, the price may change, without any corresponding change in the real value, just as by diminishing the yard measure we increase the number of yards in a piece of cloth. The cupidity and the prejudice of governments have many times prompted the alteration of the

legal standard. This has generally been done by changing the weights of the coins; as when the profligate Roman emperor Elagabulus, who was entitled to receive pieces of gold from his subjects, cunningly increased the amount of gold in the aureus;* and the kings of England, when they found their debts pressing heavily, diminished the weight of the pound sterling, in order that they might the more easily discharge them.† In modern times the change of standard has generally been effected by substituting paper for coin. In such cases ignorance and prejudice have generally dictated the total repudiation of the old standard, and the reference of all values to the new one. This has been aptly likened to "hiding the thermometer" in order to avoid the heat.

These degradations of the standard of value, in order that debts may be more easily discharged, are as gross a fraud as a diminution of the yard measure by a power which had agreed to furnish a cer-

---

* *Encyclopædia Britannica* (Art. MONEY). It is here suggested that Elagabalus took the hint from a governor of the Gauls under Augustus, who divided the year into fourteen months, instead of twelve, because the Gauls paid a certain *monthly* tribute.

† From the Norman Conquest until the reign of Edward III., the pound sterling contained a pound of silver. From that time until Edward VI., there was an almost continual degradation of the standard. It is now less than one-third its original value. But this was nothing to the doings of the House of Stuarts, in Scotland, who, in a century and a half, reduced the quantity of silver in the pound to less than one-twentieth its former amount.

tain amount of cloth, in order that he might fulfil his contract in name without doing it in deed. Why, then, have they not met with a reprobation corresponding to their criminality? The answer is obvious: a measure of value is not directly cognizable by the senses, like the length of a yard-stick. For a long time, therefore, the *name* usurps the place of the *thing*. The new "pound," "franc," or "dollar," is called by the same name as the old one; and even when every one sees that one old dollar will sell for two new ones in the market, it is difficult to conceive that this does not proceed in part from an increase in the value of the old one. The illusion can be completely eradicated only by remembering that the gold mines yield their treasures as freely as ever, and that in foreign countries the old coins are no more valuable than before. But, if the yard measure were reduced to eighteen inches, every one would see at once that the new yard was only half as long as the old one; that a piece of cloth which formerly measured thirty yards was no longer than before, although it now measured sixty; that if he had loaned thirty yards of cloth before the change of measure, he would be defrauded out of half his just due if compelled to receive thirty of the new yards as an equivalent.

4. Although, by such changes in the standard of value, the equilibrium of prices may be temporarily disturbed, this disturbance cannot be permanent. The disturbance is felt in the wholesale be-

fore being felt in the retail market; in the prices of those articles the production of which requires an easily-calculated expenditure of labor, before it is felt in those of which the labor of production cannot be exactly estimated. Sooner or later, however, all prices must change to correspond to the new standard. The price of no one article of general use can be permanently raised in this way without lifting all other prices with it. Let us take gold for example, because this is the standard to which all other standards must be referred. Suppose that every man who has a gold dollar can get two dollars in currency for it from a speculator, from his neighbor, or from any one else, while they will give him no more than before for the products of his labor. If he makes butter, flour, clocks, or any thing which we are in the habit of exporting, self-interest will make him refuse the prices offered, and export his goods, in order to receive gold for them. Thus, the price of his goods will certainly go up to correspond with gold. The prices of goods which cannot be exported must follow, because otherwise men would gradually stop making them, and turn their attention entirely to exportable commodities. Thus beginning at the stock and wholesale market, the wave would gradually roll under every class of business, until it reached the street lozenge-vender, who would charge four cents instead of two for a paper of lozenges.

The increase of prices in our country furnishes

a very good illustration of the principles laid down. Two economic theories respecting this state of things have been so widely disseminated that it is well worth while to give them a close examination. Those who hold them would probably express them as follows:

1. The rise in gold does not correctly and fairly express a depreciation of our legal standard of value, but is in part fictitious. Although a dollar note will only bring from forty to fifty cents in gold, it is really worth more. The price of every thing did not go up to correspond with gold.

2. Granting that the depreciation of the standard is real, it is the work of stock-jobbers and speculators, who have compassed the depreciation in order to forward their own selfish ends.

Perhaps the former doctrine can be most easily and conclusively refuted by an appeal to first principles. It is indisputable that men on the average can now possess themselves of a dollar in greenbacks with as much ease as they could obtain forty or fifty cents in gold before the war, barring the insignificant tax on production levied by the General Government. Every man who feeds us, every man who clothes us, nearly every one who ministers to our wants in any form, gets in return from two to three times the money he got before, without working any harder for it. The merchant makes twice as much money by buying and selling the same actual amount of goods, the butcher gets two or three times as much for his meat, and the farmer for his corn. Labor being the most natural measure of value of which we can conceive, it follows that men do not *desire* and therefore do not *value* a dollar of our present currency more than the amount of our old money which the present dollar will purchase.

It may be answered that there is no good reason for this great depreciation of the standard; that the notes are really secure, and will be as good as gold when the war ends. The only objection to this argument is, that it does not bear on the point in question. We are not concerned with the *real* value of the money, but with the estimate which the community at large set upon it. Individuals are but drops in the ocean. A few such drops may object to the tidal influence of the moon and insist on remaining on the beach while the tide recedes, but the ebb and flow will go on just the same in spite of them.

In logical strictness, the second argument, that against speculators, is irrelevant to our subject. The *cause* of the depreciation does not alter the fact, nor does it affect the consequences which flow from that fact. It is of interest to us only so far as it is under our control, and it is impossible to control speculation without entirely prohibiting all business. But the doctrine that speculation is the cause of all the disturbance has been repeatedly endorsed in such high official quarters, and has taken such deep root in the public mind, that it is worth while to analyze it. Singular as it may seem, this doctrine has been most strenuously maintained by the supporters of the paper standard, who should have been the last ones to admit it; for if such a standard is really at the mercy of a class of gamblers, this very fact would furnish the strongest argument against its adoption.

Speculation consists in buying goods in anticipation of a rise in their price, in order to make a profit by selling them after the rise. The speculator may intend to bring about the rise himself; or he may only take advantage of it without being in any way the cause of it. If the market offers but a limited supply of some indispensable article, he secretly and suddenly buys the stock on hand, and then compels the public to buy from him at his own price until a new supply can be obtained. In such a case as this the speculator is really the cause of the rise. The more necessary the article and the more limited the supply, the more easy is this operation. Gold is about the last thing in the world to be operated on in this way, because it is something which the whole world are always ready to supply, and which no one is compelled to provide himself with. The absurdity of any attempt to raise the price of gold artificially may be easily illustrated. Suppose that all the speculators in the country unite themselves into a firm for the express purpose of raising the price of gold. While the people at large are willing to sell their goods at double the gold price, this firm sets the price of gold at 250.

To make the case as favorable as possible, suppose they have got possession of all the gold in the market and refuse to sell for less than 260, while they offer 250 for all that may be brought to them. What will be the effect? A shipper has $10,000 in gold which he is about to export to England for dry goods. On seeing the speculator's offer, he modifies his venture by selling his gold to them for $25,000 in currency, with which he buys 2,000 barrels of flour at $12½ per barrel, which he exports instead of the gold. For the flour he receives $14,000 in gold, supposing the English price to be $7, which his consignee draws from the Bank of England. Importing this coin, he sells it to the speculators for $35,000, thus making from $10,000 to $15,000 clear profit by the operation. In the same way will the speculators stimulate the shipment of goods to every place where gold can be obtained, while a steady stream of that metal will flow into their coffers from the vaults of Europe and the mines of California, until their capital is exhausted. During this time the prices of all exportable goods would rise to correspond with the speculators' price of gold, if it were certain that the capital of the firm would hold out until the gold could be got from Europe. After its exhaustion, the *cause* of the great rise having ceased, gold and every thing would go down to its old price, and the speculators would be ruined, for no one would give more than 200 for gold, while goods enough to buy

$100 in gold in Europe or California can be had for less than $200 in currency.

No set of men could ever be guilty of so mad an attempt to injure the government credit, because self-interest would dissuade them from it. Human nature is exhibited in the stock market just as it is. The buyer of gold, like all other buyers, will obtain what he wants as cheaply as he can get it. If a speculator, or any one else, gives 150 per cent. premium for gold, it is only because no one in this or any other country will let him have as much as he wants of it for 149. The case has been supposed for the sake of illustrating the powerlessness of individuals to seriously alter the equilibrium of values, though controlled by the most inexplicable motives.

If measures as desperate as these would be so entirely ineffectual, still less so would be the common way of speculating, which amounts, in effect, to betting on prices. The general idea of this operation seems to be that every one bets against the Government, and no one for it; or, at least, that he who bets for it is powerless. But I trust it does not require any argument to show that for every bull there must be a bear; that the bear will have as great an interest in the fall as the bull in the rise; and that the bear's exertions to attain his end will be as powerful and as effective as those of his opponent. How, then, can their efforts change the price?

Bull and bear are in fact equally powerless to effect any great or permanent change in the price of so universal and easily transportable an article as gold. At best they can only foresee the change. The stock market registers the price of gold, but does not fix it. It is governed entirely by the relation between the supply and demand. The supply and demand are governed by public opinion, and depend entirely upon it. How, it will not be difficult to show:

1. Taking that portion of the community who have occasion to buy or sell gold, whether they be speculators, importers, manufacturers of jewelry, bankers, or owners of gold mines; if ten men of this class think gold is likely to fall, while only nine think it will rise, there will be ten sellers for nine buyers, and the price will fall, temporarily or permanently.

2. The influence of these men is small compared with that of the public generally. The effect of the opinion of the large mass of the community may be most easily appreciated by remembering that the real value of gold is subject to no appreciable change, and that the fluctuations of its price represent fluctuations in the value of legal tender notes, just as the height of a man would vary if measured by a rule of varying length. Suppose now that an Ohio farmer, who never heard of a stock board or the premium on gold, has received a hundred dollars in notes for his wheat. He knows that the

same wheat would have brought him only forty dollars in gold. If he is disposed to set a higher value on this money than his neighbors generally, he will be disposed to sell more wheat, and to spend the least possible amount of the money in buying goods at such high prices. He will either keep the money, or invest it in government bonds. The increased amount of wheat he has thrown on the market will then cause the price to fall, and his refusal to buy the usual amount of dry goods will diminish the demand for them, both effects being caused by the farmer's increased appreciation of legal tender notes. The fall in wheat will stimulate an increased export of that article, while the diminished demand for dry goods will cause a diminished importation. The importer will want less gold for foreign export, so that the price of gold also will fall.

But, suppose the farmer, through improvidence, or want of confidence in the Government, spends his money in fine clothes. He will then create a demand for five yards more of foreign broadcloth, without throwing the wheat on the market to pay for it; the importer will be found in the gold market inquiring for $20 more gold than he would otherwise want, and the price will rise.

Thus the sentiments of the Ohio farmer are reflected in the gold market. The influence of one man will of course be infinitesimal, but the influence of millions will govern it entirely. The market is a most delicate and impartial thermometer, which registers the average opinion of the country as it is manifested by men's preferences in buying and selling. The opinions will not be registered at once. They must first cause men to *act*, to buy less or sell more, and it may then be some time longer before the effect of the actions will be felt in the gold market, just as the sun is up some hours before he has warmed the air, and caused the thermometer to rise. But the rise or fall will be anticipated by those who have gold to buy or sell, according to their best judgment. The coming waves of supply and demand will be looked for with all the care of men who know that their pockets must pay for the smallest mistake.

2*

CHAPTER II.

THE FINANCIAL ELEMENTS OF MILITARY STRENGTH.

THE illusions of habit are as numerous as those of the sense. Our accustomed associations of ideas may confirm us in an erroneous theory as strongly as the senses of the untaught confirm them in the notion that the earth is flat and immovable. Men's erroneous notions respecting the functions of money are for the most part purely artificial. "The true theory of money," says Professor Bowen,* " when nakedly stated, seems like a string of paradoxes which contradict the common sense of mankind." This string hangs from another seeming paradox, that the less men have used or desired money, the more correctly they will be able to appreciate its true functions. If a tribe of savages about to undertake a raid, were advised to supply themselves beforehand with a commodity which every one desired to possess, but which could neither be made into spears nor cooked into food, they would conclude that the benefits to be derived were of supernatural origin. Their views of the natural advan-

---

* Political Economy, Chap. XVIII.

tages to be derived from such a commodity would be nearly correct, not only as applied to themselves, but to any collection of people however numerous. They would be unable to comprehend the *tableau vivant* of a late reviewer who exhibits to their astonished gaze twenty millions of people, possessed of every appliance of war, and threatened with destruction by their enemies, yet unable to move a finger, turn a wheel, or fire a musket, until they are set in motion by the beneficent invention of certain pieces of green paper.

This inability would proceed from their practical good sense. When we consider money as a source of power, we make such a mistake as a railroad engineer would who had gradually imbibed the notion that it was the rails and not the steam which moved his engine, and that fire and water were mere conveniences for keeping it in order. So long as he made the accustomed use of these conveniences no harm would result from his false theory; but if, in an emergency, he should trust to the rails alone to move his engine, he would discover his error.

When we hear poets call gold and iron the sinews of war; reviews tell how paper money drains swamps, and builds roads, ships, and cities; and popular orators call upon the people to aid the Government by converting a note which bears no interest into a bond on which Government has to pay interest in gold; we can hardly separate the poetical from the prosaic, the ideal from the real, and the figurative from the literal. Such expressions give us no deeper practical insight into the true functions of money, than figurative statements that iron rails drive the locomotive, and the yard-stick is the sinew of commerce, would add to the practical knowledge of an engineer or a merchant. Quite harmless as poetic fancies, they will be pernicious indeed as maxims to shape our policy. Gold is a sinew of war in no higher sense than quicksilver or platinum, or any thing else for which we can obtain munitions of war. Cannon foundries and fertile fields, trust in God; and a consciousness of right; these are the real sinews of war. Without them, the gold fields of California will be useless; with them, gold will never be wanted.

But money has its uses. In commerce it is the medium of exchange, for which every man sells, and with which he buys. Its use in war can be best seen by beginning with the requirements of war itself. In what does the military power of a nation consist? Undoubtedly in the magnitude and courage of its armies, the efficiency of its artillery, and its power of making good the waste of war. That nation which can cast most shot and shell, transport them to the seat of war with the greatest facility, and project them in the greatest numbers, will possess in the greatest degree the material elements of military strength. Its efficiency in these respects will depend on the efficiency of its mines, its foundries, and its machine shops, its agriculture and its manufactures of clothing. This, again, will depend on the number of men that can be spared from the pursuits of peace to dig coal and iron, cast shell, make wagons and clothing in the mines and shops already built, and to dig new mines, and build new shops. If it is stored with no minerals, the men who would otherwise be engaged in digging coal and iron may be employed perhaps with equal advantage in producing food and clothing, to be exchanged for coal and iron with other countries; and unless it is capable of employing its industry in this way, it will be unable to wage war. Hence we derive the fundamental proposition:

The military power of a nation is measured by the amount of industry which it can divert into the channels of war.

This proposition will be universally admitted. It is equally true in ancient and in modern times. The great point of difference between the ancient and modern systems, which makes a budget more necessary to the latter than to the former powers, is simply this: in ancient times almost the only labor which was necessary to the prosecution of war was that of the soldier who did the fighting; while with us, nearly every branch of human industry is in some way made subservient to the preservation and efficiency of the army. The iron-founders, the miners, the carpenters, the ship-builders, the chemists, the surgeons, are all called upon to contribute their labor, and indirectly to fight the iron-founders and ship-builders of the other side. The success of the cause depends as much on the skill displayed by these professions as upon the courage of the soldiers.

The question now is, Does money increase the amount of skill and labor which can be thus turned into the channels of war? I answer, No; although on a cursory view it might seem that the question should be answered in the affirmative. It may be pronounced impossible for industry to be diverted into the channels of war without the aid of money. The manufacturers cannot supply the army with clothing, unless they receive money with which to pay their operatives and keep their machinery in repair. The soldiers must be paid, else their families will starve. All this seems very reasonable; but let us look at the question a little closer.

What the nation really wants is *labor*, a certain number of days' work from every inhabitant. If there were no money, taxes would have to be paid in this shape. If one-tenth of the productive population were entirely engaged in the war, then the remaining nine-tenths would have to be called upon for one-tenth of the product of their labor. The manufacturer would give one-tenth of the cloth he made; this would be handed to the tailor, who would be required to spend one day in ten in making it into clothes. The farmer would give a tithe of his harvest, which would suffice to feed every one in Government employ. By such a system of taxation the war would be as efficiently, though not so conveniently, supported without the money as with it. The inconveniences would be these: The tax might not be entirely equable; for less than one-tenth of some products, and far more of others, would be needed. One factory might be in an inconvenient position for supplying the army, and besides have some other very profitable contract on hand; while another might be conveniently situated, and have nothing to do but supply the Government. Clearly, then, it will tend most to the public good if the latter can be employed exclusively upon Government account; and nine-tenths of its work be paid for by others. *Money* enables this to be done in such a way that every one shall be taxed equally. Government demands from the individual, not labor, but money, which is the representative of labor. With the money thus obtained, it enters the market and purchases its supplies on the best terms that it can obtain.

It is very plain, however, that the Government cannot obtain any money by taxes or loans, unless the payers can earn more than they need for their own consumption; nor will there be any supplies in the market unless more goods are manufactured than are needed by the country at large. Let us suppose that our soil were so poor, our manufactures so rude, and our wants so numerous, that the entire products of our industry are required to supply those wants. Our farmers can only raise food enough to feed us, the factories can only make cloth enough to clothe us, and we have no idle population to devote to the manufacture of war materials. In such a case, no amount of money, paper or metallic, would enable us to wage war. We could not spare a farmer to take the field, because his fellow farmers could not then raise food to subsist themselves and him too; we could not spare a manufacturer to cast shot, or build a powder mill, because the manufacturers who are left could not then make the necessary amount of clothes. The Government could buy nothing, because there would be nothing to buy, though it possessed the silver mines of Peru.

It may be replied, that in such a case the offer of articles which men desire so strongly as silver and gold, would stimulate them to extraordinary efforts in the production and manufacture of war material, and to extraordinary self-denial in the consumption of food and clothing. Very true; but it would only increase their *willingness*, not their *ability*, to work extra hours, and stint themselves in the enjoyment of the necessaries of life. The willingness is indeed as important to the Government as the ability, but we are at present considering the power which a nation *can* exert, not what it *will* exert. Besides, even the increased willingness depends on the supposition that the Government has obtained possession of the precious metals without taxing the people, which is a case that does not often occur in practice. It seems, then, *that the amount of industry which a people can divert into the channels of war is not increased by the possession of any sort of money. The latter only facilitates the diversion by making it easier to measure each man's share of the public burden.*

An attempt, on the part of a community, to make military efforts beyond its strength, is productive of certain well-defined effects which we shall proceed to show.

The Government levies taxes, and raises loans in gold, with which it hopes to purchase supplies for its armies. It purchases from a manufacturer clothing which the latter would otherwise exchange for bread. In lieu of the clothing he must now offer gold for his bread. It also purchases from the farmer corn which he would otherwise exchange for clothing, so that the farmer must now offer gold for his clothing instead of corn. Clothing, bread, and every thing else required for the army, will, in consequence, become scarce and dear; and gold will be exported by the people to supply the want. Then comes general distress among the poorer classes, and general scarcity of money.

If, now, the Government attempts to remedy the scarcity of money by prohibiting the export of specie and by issuing paper money, the consequence will be a universal rise in the prices of the necessaries required by the people and the army, so that neither the distress nor the scarcity will be mitigated in any degree. If the paper money is redeemable in coin on demand, the rise will not be so rapid as if it is not so redeemable. In the latter case, it will speedily lose all purchasing power, no matter how secure may be its ultimate redemption; for the simple reason that people cannot afford to part with the fruits of labor for any thing but necessaries.

Thus, the inevitable effect of the attempt alluded to will be universal distress among the poorer classes, accompanied either by enormous prices or great scarcity of money, according as the policy of the Government has or has not tended to expand the currency. The distress, and the difficulty of procuring supplies, will, for the time being, be entirely independent of the financial policy of the government, following equally whether the war be carried on with paper or with gold, by loans or by taxation. We have seen them in France in the time of the revolution; in England during the Napoleonic wars; and we see them in the rebel states now. They are the true and only indications that the resources of the country are taxed to the utmost.

It might have been possible to make the love of gold the means of demoralizing, and finally destroying, the Southern Confederacy. If, during the war, we had allowed the rebels to export what they pleased, without restriction, receiving in exchange therefor nothing but gold, what would have been the consequence? Individuals, instead of devoting themselves to the poorly paid task of supplying the rebel government, would have exerted all their energies in raising cotton, to export for gold. The possession of this metal would have been a source of great gratification to the individual owners, but would have added nothing to the military strength of the rebel government. The policy would, therefore, have acted as a bribe to devote their energies to other purposes than the prosecution of war. The only objection to it would be that much of the gold would have fallen into the hands of the rebel government, and been employed in fitting out privateers in foreign countries.

We have now arrived at a standpoint where we can clearly see what the measure of military power really is. It depends upon, and is measured by the excess of what the nation is able to produce over and above what is necessary for its subsistence. If all our labor is exhausted in the production of food, clothing, and other necessaries, we cannot make war at all, as we have already seen. If half our labor is sufficient for this purpose; if one-half our productive population can, by their industry, supply the whole; we can then employ the entire energies of the other half in war. On an average every man can spend half his time either in fighting or making things to fight with.

But we make a great mistake when, as is often done, we estimate this excess of production over consumption by its actual amount in time of peace. This only shows what we can spend in war without working any harder than usual, and without depriving ourselves of any enjoyment that costs money or labor. But there is generally a large, partially idle population which can be employed in case of an emergency; men can work more industriously, and they can greatly curtail their expenditures.

All we have said of the source of military strength may be concentrated into one word, Frugality. It is the frugal man who consumes less than he produces; and as the nation is made up of individuals, it is the frugal nation which can turn its energies to war, and at the same time supply its own wants. It is the frugal nation which in time of peace will be prepared for war. On the other hand, the man who consumes all that he produces will never have any thing to sell the Government, no matter how much money the Government may have to pay with; and a nation composed entirely of such individuals will not only be unprepared for war, but will have to change its habits before it can prepare.

Thus the trite maxim, which men are generally so much more ready to apply to others than to themselves, namely, that one's wealth is measured by the simplicity of his wants as much as by the amount of his income is the expression of a great and important political truth. A nation may be saved or destroyed according as its people are willing or unwilling to dispense with costly luxuries.

That the labor of engines, as well as of men, is to be included in the war power; that foundries, mines, and machine shops all add to military strength; that the nation which already possesses cannon, means of transportation, and military stores in quantities sufficient for the war, will have a great advantage over one which has yet to cast its cannon and build its wagons; all this is too evident to require further elucidation. Wealth in all these forms is power. But there other phases of the problem which are very difficult. Wealth is not always power; in some respects it may be absolute weakness. There are, in fact, two entirely different points of view from which the science of the accumulation of wealth may be approached; and according as we take one view or another of the objects of human industry we shall be led to different answers to the question, What ought a nation to do with its money?

Political economy, as an abstract science, considers every thing as wealth which men desire, and which they can obtain by labor, and in no other way. It does not discuss the ethical question whether men *ought* to desire it; the bare fact that men *do* desire it, and are willing to labor in order to enjoy it, is all that concerns it. The value of any article of wealth is measured by the least amount of labor adequate to its possession by the individual who desires it. If a laborer is willing to work all day for a quart of whiskey to get drunk upon, political economy does not question his wisdom; it argues that the quart of whiskey must afford him more enjoyment than any thing else he could obtain at the same price, else he would have bought something else. Any law or regulation which forces him to buy any thing else detracts from his welfare, which is looked upon as one and the same thing with the utmost gratification of his wishes.

If all men really desired their highest good at all times, no fault could be found with any of the conclusions of this pure science. But such is not the case; and it is the part of statesmanship to encourage those desires which really tend to good, and to discourage those which tend toward evil. When it is once concluded what desires are good, and what are evil, political economy steps in as a concrete science, and shows how the good may be encouraged, and the evil discouraged. The question to be solved then is, how must our labor be employed to promote our welfare in the greatest degree?

In the present chapter we are entirely employed with this question. The national good which we are supposed to be seeking is neither wealth nor the utmost gratification of our desires, but military power. It may, indeed, be considered as an application of the principles of political economy to the case of a nation whose great desire is to attain the largest measure of military strength. A discussion of the entire subject might fill a volume; we are at present trying to discover what financial condition is most conducive to this end. Particularly are we seeking to discover the functions of the precious metals in enabling a nation to carry on war. It has, I hope, been made sufficiently plain that the possession of gold adds no more to the internal power of a nation, no matter how large, than a silver mine would have added to the resources of Robinson Crusoe. The sole office of money is to *equalize* the burden of war among the individual citizens; and this can be done as effectually by a correct system of paper money as by exchanges of gold. But, every gold dollar is the embodiment and expression of a certain amount of war material which the possessor can command in foreign countries. To command the material it is necessary to export the dollar. The latter has, then, disappeared; in its place has appeared a musket, or a box of percussion caps. It is certain, then, that, other conditions being equal, the nation which has the most gold can make the greatest military efforts, because a people can always export readily their entire stock of gold without serious detriment to their business, or their enjoyment. This metal is thus a reservoir of power. But a collection of any other sort of property, equally desired by mankind at large, and equally transportable, would be equally a reservoir of power. The only reasons why quicksilver or platinum would not be as good as gold, are, in the first place, that equal values of them cannot be transported so easily; and in the next place, that the demand for them is so far from universal that their value would be diminished by throwing any considerable amount on the market at once. It is probable that fifty millions of dollars' worth of gold would find a more ready market in any European country than ten millions' worth of any other article.

Is it, then, desirable to encourage the accumulation of the precious metals in time of prosperity, in order that we may have them to fall back upon in time of adversity? It is impossible to answer this question absolutely, because it depends on the habits, dispositions, and circumstances of the nation. But we can easily lay out the foundation on which it depends. It must be remembered that there is one objection, and only one, to such accumulation; the loss of interest on the capital thus accumulated. Gold and silver coin is, in the strictest sense, unproductive capital, whether lying in the vaults of banks, or locked up in a miser's chest, or circulating as money. Every man who has it in his possession loses the interest during the time it remains so, as will be quite clear on reflecting that no one would pay interest on gold to *keep*, but only to exchange as soon as possible for something else. Hence, the use of the precious metals as the principal currency of a nation, is deprecated by political economists. But, it must be remembered that the community, in precisely the same way, loses the interest on all the products of its labor while they are waiting to be consumed. The goods kept for sale represent so much idle capital, in the same way, and to the same extent, as does the gold kept in the vaults of a bank. If it is, on the average, a year from the time that a piece of cloth is manufactured until it finally reaches the person who is to wear it in the form of a coat, the last seller must add one year's interest to the price. If a merchant, on the average, holds his stock of goods a year before finding a purchaser, he must, in addition to every thing else, add a year's interest to the price. If cloth, like gold, was all of one kind and quality, a kind of cloth banking would be speedily introduced. In the cloth bank both the manufacturers and tailors of an entire city could deposit their goods free of expense, exactly as they deposit money in a bank, and receive a certificate that A, B, or bearer, is entitled to —— yards of cloth at the Clothiers' Bank. The bank, thus holding permanently the entire stock in trade of all the tailors of a city, could safely sell three-fourths, or even nine-tenths of it, and invest the money in dividend-paying securities. The remainder would be kept as a reserve, like the specie reserve of a money bank. As fast as one man sent in checks for his cloth, another would come in with a new deposit; and if, on any extraordinary occasion, the drafts should exceed the new deposits by an amount greater than the cloth reserve, the securities could be changed back for cloth without serious loss.

In the same way, if a nation during peace manufactures arms and munitions of war, to be kept for use in case of hostilities, it loses the interest on all the money thus spent during the time that the arms are waiting to be used, with the additional disadvantage that they may be superseded by some improved weapon. Indeed, every thing which enables the business of the nation to be carried on, and its strength to be kept intact with a diminished amount of circulating capital, whether in the form of gold kept in reserve, food waiting to be eaten, goods waiting to be sold, or arms waiting to be used, saves the amount of that diminution to the nation, and enables it to enjoy, to an additional extent, the fruits of its labor. Thus, from a politico-economic point of view, every contrivance which enables men to live "from hand to mouth" increases their wealth. The paradoxical character of this view will disappear on applying the principle to the case of an individual. If a householder is obliged, from any cause, to keep on hand continually ten barrels of flour for the use of his family, the removal of this cause will enable him to get along with only one barrel of flour at a time, and will set free, for other uses, the money formerly invested in nine barrels of flour.

But it is clear that all this utilizing of capital, while it adds to the enjoyment of the community, detracts from its power to meet a sudden emergency. Where the amount of idle capital is reduced to its minimum, there will be less coin to place at the disposal of the Government; less cloth to clothe an army; less flour to feed it; fewer muskets to arm it. But these evils will not be serious, if the utilized capital has been invested in such a form that it can be rapidly transformed into the required food, clothing, and arms. The whole problem, then, depends on this question: *What will be done with the capital set free in the ways suggested? If we do not allow gold to accumulate, what will we accumulate in place of it?* A representative case is that of the man who has been keeping ten barrels of flour on hand. Whether he sell nine of his barrels at once, or save the money he would otherwise have spent in flour, until the nine barrels are eaten up, he will have the price of nine barrels, say $50, to dispose of. If, now, he is going to spend this money in building a cannon foundry, or digging a mine, the transformation will increase the military power of the community, and ought therefore to be encouraged. But if he spend it in giving a feast to his friends, it will all have disappeared next day, and the country will be less able to feed an army, owing to the disappearance of the nine barrels of flour.

The same principle is illustrated in the case of the precious metals. To the question: Ought we to keep the gold in the country or export it? the only philosophical answer is: that depends altogether on what you get in exchange for it. If you get something which is of special importance—if in time of war you get arms and ammunition, or, in time of peace, get things which will be sources of wealth and power in the future, then by all means export it. But, if you are to receive only articles of luxury, which will be consumed without adding to your real welfare, then keep it at home. The stock of gold is like a cistern of water kept by a family against a time of drought. If this emergency is never to come, it is foolish to save the water. If it does come, it will defeat the purpose of saving the water to say that the family must still avoid drinking it. But we must distinguish between its legitimate use and its use by the children to drive a toy water-wheel.

We, therefore, conclude that it is more conducive to power to hoard our wealth than to consume it; and better still to place it in such a form that it may help to create more wealth. In more ways than one is frugality at the bottom of national as well as individual prosperity. It may not at first sight appear that he who loans his money to a manufacturer adds any more to the national wealth than if he spent it in wine and cigars; but in the former case he perhaps enables a manufacturer to enlarge his buildings and add a new engine to his works. He is *really* the *owner* of the additional power, which the manufacturer himself only uses. The latter holds himself in readiness to resign either this or its equivalent in money when the debt is demanded. When the Government is in need of military power the creditor can assign to it his debt, or, in other words, the right to use the factory power without any shock to his own business, and without giving his debtor any just cause of complaint. The Government then has command, for war purposes, of enginery which would not have been in existence but for the fact that the owner of the spare money preferred a future to a present good. It follows that the habit of frugality is as necessary in preparing for war as in carrying it on. It is the bounden duty of every government which seeks the happiness of posterity, to encourage frugality by giving all possible security to the savings of the poor. Who can measure the total additions to our war resources made by the savings banks of Massachusetts?

Thus, in whatever way we approach the subject, we are led to the strictly logical conclusion that the great and permanent elements of real power are to be found in the characters of the people, and not in the iron and gold they may possess. History teems with illustrations of the truth of this conclusion. How did Tyre, and Phœnicia, and Athens make themselves felt over a large part of the known world? How did the little republic of Venice resist the armies of Continental Europe? How did the Dutch Republic foil the mighty efforts of Louis XIV. to compass its destruction, and at the same time contest the supremacy of the ocean with the combined fleets of France and England? By their mines of iron and gold, their fertile fields, or their internal financial system? It cannot be, for in all these respects their neighbors had the advantage.

By what means have the inhabitants of the British isles been enabled to found an empire which encircles the globe? Is there any thing in the situation or resources of those little islands, not so large as New England, which has given them this enormous power? In fine, how is it that small nations have so often become great maritime powers, and that once become so, they have exerted so great an influence over the destiny of the human race? Since these effects are not due to the advantages of the position in which nature placed them, they must be due to the characteristics of the people themselves.

The fundamental cause of all this greatness is a disposition to labor for a higher good than present gratification. A luxurious people, not desirous to leave their country or the world any better than they found it, would never subject themselves to the privations and hardships of long sea voyages. We have shown that the desire of a higher good than present gratification, and the disposition to labor for that end, are the foundations of all military power; and thus it is that such people as we have alluded to have always been powerful.

Again, to launch a ship on the seemingly illimitable ocean and trust for success to the fitful action of the elements, requires both courage and skill. Without confident courage, the feat would never be attempted; without skill, it would result in the destruction of the adventurer.

The world seems designed to encourage and foster these higher qualities of the human mind by furnishing all men with the means of using them. Brains have always in the end triumphed over brute force, however fiercely the latter may have maintained the contest. The inflexible will is stronger than brass, and genius better than gold. Farragut and Bailey have shown that iron hearts within make the best plating for a ship of war. Genius, courage, honesty—above all, self-denial—these, and these alone, mould the institutions of posterity.

Necessarily following, from the notion that money is a sinew of war, is another: that a nation which has reached the point of financial exhaustion will have to stop fighting. The example of the rebellious States ought to have dispelled this illusion; for they had scarcely any financial resources worthy the name to start with, and what they had were exhausted in the beginning. Nevertheless we still find one set of men counting up the enormous sums of *money* we are spending, and another the enormous sums which our resources will enable us to pay. "We have spent $3,000,000,000 in this war," say the former. Admit that we have, where, let me ask, has this $3,000,000,000 come from? And where has it gone to? We only had from $250,000,000 to $300,000,000 of coin in the beginning, and the chances are that we have three-fourths of that amount still. Have our farmers curtailed their crops? Have they got fewer ploughs, horses, barns, or wagons than in the beginning? Are their facilities for raising horses and the means of our mechanics to build barns and make ploughs lessened? Have our factories been suffered to disappear, our engines to wear out, or our mines to fill up? I trow not. I think we possess as much material wealth as at the beginning of the war, and perhaps much more. Our unworthy financial policy has indeed caused large sums to change hands unjustly, and caused us to lose largely in that moral wealth which is so much better than material wealth, but of this hereafter. We at present want to know what is meant by saying that we have spent $3,000,000,000, when we are as rich as ever. Plainly it means neither more nor less than this, that the people of the loyal States have done $3,000,000,000 worth of work in carrying on the war. They have ploughed and reaped, and cast cannon, and rolled iron plates to this amount. If one day's work is worth on the average $3, then each man has done on the average one hundred days' work to transmit social liberty to his posterity. Is the expenditure of this labor to be regretted to the same extent that we would regret the loss of an equivalent of wealth? The answer to this question is very much a matter of taste. From a strictly economic point of view we should be compelled to answer in the affirmative. But it by no means follows that we are any poorer than if the war had not occurred. Does any one suppose that all the labor we have spent in this way would have been spent in adding to our wealth if the war had not occurred? Assuredly not. One-half would have been dedicated to idleness, or the gratification of the moment, and perhaps half the remainder to objects which every one would admit to add little or nothing to our highest good.

The point in question, as well as the difference between the highest good and the good of the political economist, may be illustrated by a single instance. An individual of dramatic tastes would spend $1 in money and three hours of time in seeing a play. The gratification he is to derive from this source must compensate him for his time and money, else he would not spend them in this way. But Government steps in with a tax, and compels him to give up his surplus dollar for the public good, and requires him to spend his three spare hours in making cartridges. Next day the Government is more powerful by one box of cartridges, worth perhaps $1, and $1 worth of munitions of war, while the individual who made the contribution is as wealthy as if it had not been required of him. As far as we may say that this diversion of labor and money is to be deplored, just so far may we deplore the expenses of war. As far as we can call it spending $2, so far may we say we have spent $3,000,000,000 in carrying on the present war.

The question we ought ask is not whether what we have gained by the war is worth so many dollars, but whether it is worth a year's work from every able-bodied man in the country.

But for our unsound financial system we might be able to continue the war for generations without seriously crippling our powers. We could not, indeed, enjoy quite so many luxuries; we could not develop our resources so rapidly; the digging of our mines and the clearing of our forests would be impeded; but we should enjoy more luxuries than our ancestors even a half century back could enjoy in time of peace. In one respect, indeed, we could not continue the war on its present scale; it is not likely that we should be able to keep half a million of effective soldiers in the field fighting such battles as have hitherto characterized the war. In all other ways we can continue our present exertions indefinitely.

The Southern States furnish an example of a people who, while commanding few of the elements of military power we have described, were nevertheless able to turn those few into the channels of war with great ease. They consumed nearly all they produced, but they spent much more in the luxuries of life than in its necessaries. Subsisting on the coarsest and cheapest food, such as a Lowell operative would have starved upon, the greater part of their wealth was devoted to the social circle, the chase, the turf, and the tournament. All these expenses are easily dispensed with, and the wealth diverted into other channels. It needs only the general acquiescence of the community to enable every one to reduce his social wants, including the luxuries of dress, to a minimum, and this acquiescence was granted by Southern society at an early period, while we are nearly as luxurious as ever. The excitements of war furnish a very good substitute for the great amusements of the Southron, but are ill-adapted to the more refined and intellectual taste of the North. Thus the transition from peace to war was accompanied with a far greater shock to the North than to the South.

Let us recapitulate some of the conclusions of this chapter.

Neither metallic nor paper money adds any thing to the *internal* power of a people.

But gold is a source of power which can be commanded by exporting the gold.

It is more conducive to military strength to put our wealth in the form of gold laid up against an emergency than to consume it.

But it is still better to put our wealth into such a form that it shall be productive of more wealth; for example, to employ it in building mills and digging mines. Such employment of our surplus means is in the greatest possible degree conducive to national strength.

CHAPTER III.

OUR DEBT AND OUR TAXES.

In the last chapter we considered the nation as, in the fullest sense of the term, a commonwealth. We considered the strength of the nation as the aggregate strength of the citizens composing it. We measured what individuals could do to promote the public welfare, not what Government might require of them. If the public good were the first and greatest object of every man's desire; if we could rely upon every man to promote that good to the utmost extent of his power, without cavilling about his just share, the question of ways and means would be a very simple one.

But such is not human nature. Every civilized man demands that his share of the public burden shall be fixed by law, and he then contributes in obedience to such law. We propose now to examine the relation of the individual to the State, and show the working of that system of governmental machinery by which every man, however peaceful his pursuits, and however difficult the division of his property, is made to contribute his equitable share toward the supply of the army with those things necessary to its efficiency. It has been shown that by demanding the required contributions in the form of money, leaving every man at liberty to obtain the money in the easiest way he can, and then buying in the cheapest market with the money, the work of carrying on the war will be distributed in the most advantageous manner. Under ordinary circumstances the privilege of paying the contribution in money offers a great advantage to the tax-payer. A still greater advantage is attained by the modern system of borrowing, provided that the Government can borrow on favorable terms. The tax-payer is then allowed to make his contribution in small sums during a long period instead of paying it all at once.

The object of the present chapter is to discuss the question whether the means for the further prosecution of the war should be raised by loans or taxation. What are the advantages and disadvantages of a national debt? Why have any national debt at all? Cannot the means necessary for the prosecution of the war be raised by taxation as advantageously as by loans? These questions are worthy of the gravest consideration, not only by our statesmen, but by the people at large. Let us consider them in their order.

When the national debt of Great Britain was increasing at the rate of forty millions sterling annually, economists were not wanting who held that such a burden must speedily prove ruinous to the financial interests of the empire. They made a mistake similar to that we make when we say we have spent $3,000,000,000 in the present war, forgetting that this expenditure has been contributed in the form of labor, not money. They forgot that this debt was not like one due from one nation to another, but was all due to the British people, as well as due by the British people, and that the public creditors would directly or indirectly pay a large portion of the debt.

The debt went on until it reached nearly £1,000,000,000 sterling, and the British empire not only still preserved its vigour, but went on growing as rapidly as ever. An error of an opposite character then began to pervade the public mind. The increase of wealth and power continuing in spite of the debt, the latter was concluded to be the cause of the increase. Men gradually came to consider it the great consolidating power which gives strength and permanency to the empire. The payment of the debt depending on the continuance of the Government, every one who holds a share in the public stocks is thought to have an interest to the full amount of that share in the permanence of the Government. It has been attempted to reason in the same way with respect to the debt which we are accumulating with such unexampled rapidity. Let us see, therefore, what foundation there really is for such an opinion, and how far the reasoning is applicable to our case.

Every one who holds government bonds draws from the Government interest on the bonds, and it is therefore to his advantage that the Government should be preserved. But whence comes the money which pays the interest? Does Government create it? Not at all; it must raise the entire amount by taxation. The taxpayers therefore have, altogether, as great an interest in the destruction of the Government as the public creditors have in its continuance, since as much money is raised by taxes as is paid out in interest. The whole reasoning falls to the ground, unless it is shown that the bondholders exert more political power than the taxpayers. In England this is undoubtedly the case, for three reasons:

1. Political power is there nearly proportional to wealth. The public creditors, belonging, for the most part, to the more wealthy and influential classes of the community, hold in their own hands a large share of the political power of the country. The taxes, being mostly levied on the products of labor, a considerable portion of them are in reality paid by those who have no voice in the affairs of Government.

2. The taxes being to a great extent indirect are less felt than if they were drawn directly from the pockets of those who really pay them.

3. Finally, the sentiment of justice will always

be felt to demand the continued payment of the debt.

Now, while the last two causes may operate as strongly in this country as in England, the first will not. Here, wealth endows its possessors with less political power than there. In theory it here endows them with no power at all, since no amount of wealth gives its possessor more than one vote. Our taxpayers will have half a dozen votes to our bondholders one; and this state of things will offer the unprincipled politician a tempting field in which to aggrandize himself by fostering and advocating the principles of agrarianism. If, indeed, every tax-payer could be induced to take such a share of the public debt that he should receive in interest as much as he paid in taxes, we should have nothing to fear from this cause. But the idea of such a division is chimerical. Even if effected, it would not be permanent. The debt would rapidly flow out of the hands of the improvident into those of the frugal; from the hands of the poor into those of the rich; from the business man to the professional man.

This is not the worst; it will inevitably gravitate toward particular sections, on exactly the same principles. It will leave those sections where agricultural, manufacturing, and mining capital is scarce, and accumulate in those sections where it is plenty. The debt which is held in the West will flow East in exchange for agricultural implements, steam machinery, and the products of our looms and our anvils. Or, which amounts to the same thing, it will come East in exchange for manufactured articles on which the Western men will subsist while they are erecting the mills and factories and digging the mines which are to be the future sources of their wealth. In the East, where the mills and factories are already built, and engaged in actively competing with each other; where, therefore, the rate of interest and profit on capital is lower, the bonds will be relatively more valuable, for the same reason that 3 per cent. consols are worth twice as much in England as they would be in this country.

Thus, in a very few years, four-fifths of our debt will almost certainly be held in the Atlantic States, while more than half the taxes will have to be paid by the States which own the other fifth. Holding, as the latter will, more than half the political power, how long before they will forget the mills, and factories, and fences for which they have exchanged the debt? How long before we shall see a race of ambitious and unprincipled demagogues seeking to ride into power by advocating some policy by which the Western people may be relieved of the taxes which they will be paying to the people of other States? If we have to wait long for these things there will be a most gratifying improvement in public honesty. Considering the danger of such a result, it must be admitted that our debt, if suffered to increase any further, is more likely to prove an element of weakness by causing an antagonism of interests between the East and the West, than to prove an element of strength by giving the public creditors an interest in the continuance of the Government. The attempt to apply the English argument to this country furnishes one instance out of many of the danger of applying the argument from analogy without due consideration of the differences as well as the likenesses of the things compared. We see that an argument perfectly legitimate when applied to a consolidated Government and homogeneous people like those of England, may prove entirely delusive if applied to a heterogeneous country like our own, different sections of which may have entirely different pecuniary interests.

Yet another argument frequently urged in favor of raising money for an important war by loans instead of taxes, is that the burden of the war is thus partially thrown upon posterity, for whose benefit it is fought. But we must ask leave to dispute the doctrine that the burden of war or any other labor performed by one generation can be thrown on another by any means whatever. The generation that wages the war must be the one to shed its blood, feed its armies, and cast the shot and shell which its armies are to use. Food, clothing, shot and shell are the real expenses of war. In running into debt for these articles, we do indeed bequeath to posterity the work of raising the money to pay for them. But posterity not only raises the money, but also receives the pay, so that we may as logically say that posterity gets paid for the war as to say that it pays for it. The descendants of those who have done less than their share pay the descendants of those who have done more; but the total amount of wealth inherited is about the same, whether their forefathers carried on the war by loans or taxes.

Supposing it equally easy to raise money by loans and by taxes, these two reasons are, it is believed, the only sound and forcible ones for preferring the former plan. We have shown that one does not apply to this country at all, and that the other has no logical foundation. We are now prepared to discuss the question from a purely financial point of view; that is, to consider the relative burdens imposed on industry by the two systems. And here let me say that our erroneous views of the reasons why a national debt should be incurred at all, are at the bottom of all our financial mistakes, and are the fruitful source of all the difficulties which our treasury has had to encounter? Why might we not have raised every dollar we needed for the prosecution of the war by taxes? No doubt a large majority of readers will say, "Because it was impossible to raise such large sums by taxation. The attempts to do so would paralyze industry, and thus defeat the very object aimed at. We cannot possibly raise $1,000,000,000 by taxation in a single year."

This doctrine seems to be so firmly rooted in the public mind, that the raising of nearly all our war expenses by loans has been considered an imperious necessity. To this supposed necessity we have patiently submitted, under all circumstances, without once inquiring whether it was real or imaginary.

In opposition to this popular view it is claimed that a national debt is only a choice of evils, and that under our present circumstances the debt is a greater evil than its alternative. In support of this I appeal to history. The very idea of a funded national debt is a modern one. Nations have waged war in all ages on a scale as grand as ours in comparison with their resources without seeking to burden the future. It is not likely that either Alexander, Cæsar, or Charlemagne, ever borrowed money. True, in ancient times war could be carried on with less expense than now, owing to the simplicity of the equipments of an army; but the ability of the people to pay taxes was less in a still larger ratio. Besides, modern warfare has also been conducted on the largest scale without borrowing as we do. Neither Louis XIV. nor Charles V. ever incurred a permanent debt. The most they did was to anticipate their revenue by issuing exchequer bills, or giving the public creditors a lien on particular taxes.

Indeed, the rate at which we are borrowing has no precedent in the history of nations. The greatest loans ever attempted even by Great Britain, are insignificant when compared with ours. During the first sixteen years of the present century, when that power was engaged in the most gigantic efforts which her history has recorded, she only borrowed, on an average, £22,000,000 sterling, or $106,000,000 per annum, and the greatest amount ever borrowed in one year was less than $200,000,000. These loans only sufficed to pay the interest on the debt previously contracted, so that *her entire war expenses during her struggle with Napoleon were sustained by taxation.* We are now borrowing at the rate of $600,000,000 per annum. Moreover, as the real burden of the debt is to be measured by the interest and not by the principal, and as we are paying half as much interest again as England did, it follows that we are practically running into debt eight or ten times as fast as England did during the wars with Napoleon.*

* In the beginning of 1801, the public debt of Great Britain amounted to £528,000,000. The following table shows in round numbers the sums borrowed in each subsequent year, allowing for the excess of exchequer bills issued over those redeemed:

    1801, £28,000,000 = $136,000,000
    1802, £21,000,000 = $102,000,000
    1803, £15,000,000 = $73,000,000
    1804, £18,000,000 = $87,000,000
    1805, £20,000,000 = $97,000,000
    1806, £18,000,000 = $87,000,000
    1807, £12,000,000 = $58,000,000
    1808, £15,000,000 = $73,000,000
    1809, £17,000,000 = $82,000,000
    1810, £13,000,000 = $63,000,000

· But the claim needs no appeal to history to substantiate it. The very fact that we have spent $1,000,000,000, a year in war, without producing any sensible increase in the values* of goods without driving all our gold out of the country, and without causing any general distress among the poor, does of itself furnish the most conclusive proof that we could have raised this amout by some system of taxation. We have seen in the last chapter that when we say we have spent all this money, we only mean that individuals of the nation have done $1,000,000,000 worth of work for the Government. We have also seen that the possession

   1811, £21,000,000 = $102,000,000
   1812, £29,000,000 = $140,000,000
   1813, £24,000,000 = $116,000,000
   1814, £26,000,000 = $126,000,000
   1815, £21,000,000 = $102,000,000

   Total, £298,000,000=$1,244,000,000

During the last three years about £37,000,000 additional was borrowed and loaned to foreign Powers, making a total increase of the national debt of £335,000,000, or $1,621,000,000 during the fifteen years; a little more than half the debt we have incurred in four years.

The average rate of interest was generally about five per cent. on the sums actually paid into the treasury. The notion that the money was borrowed on unfavorable terms, because the debt contracted was frequently in excess of the sums received, is founded on a misapprehension. Five per cent. stock was nearly always worth par; and it was when the rate of interest was only three per cent. on the nominal par value of the stock, that £100 of the latter was exchanged for £60 in money.

 * By the "value of goods" is meant their *gold* value, and not their market *price* measured by the depreciating, uncertain, and ever varying standard which the legal tender act has authorized.

of money adds nothing to the amount of work which individuals can do for the Government. At the worst, then, this labor could all have been demanded as commutation for a special war tax. Let us, however, go further into details.

It has already been shown that the only possible way in which a nation can equip an army from its own resources is by turning a certain amount of its industry into the channels of war; that the military power of the nation is measured by the amount of industry which can be thus diverted; and that the amount depends on the ability of the people to do more than supply their own wants. We have also seen that money does not increase the power of diverting labor, but only furnishes a means of making every individual do his just share.

Suppose, now, that we wish to devote one-fourth of the entire productive power of the country into the channels of war; in other words, that we consider it necessary to employ one-fourth of the entire productive population in the manufacture of war material. We then levy a tax of 25 per cent. on the entire production of the country. One-fourth the breadstuffs raised by the farmer will feed the government employés, with their wives and children. One-fourth the products of the looms will clothe them. In fine, the required fourth being paid the Government in the form of money, that money will enable the government employés not in the field to enjoy, on the average, the same comforts that the remaining three-fourths of the community do.

Can the productive population spare one-fourth of all they produce, and still have enough left for themselves? Yes: *because they actually do it.* At least one-fourth of our productive population is actually engaged in carrying on the war, yet our farmers do raise enough to feed them, and our factories to clothe them. The only essential respect in which the plan marked out differs from that actually adopted is this: instead of demanding the required fourth as a *tax* we accept it as a loan, giving the producer promissory notes labelled " United States will pay " in exchange therefor. As this note does not minister to any bodily want, the nation at large is none the richer for its issue.

Another objection has more weight. Would not so heavy a tax discourage industry, and lead men to give up producing every thing not absolutely essential to their subsistence? This question can be answered only by judging from experience and analogy. In recent times, we have no example of so heavy a tax. But it would, in its effects on industry, be precisely similar to a forcible deprivation of such portion of our mechanical power, and labor-saving machines, that men would have to do one-third more labor to produce the same amount of goods. As an example, take the production of wheat. Suppose that by the use of sowing, reaping, and threshing machines, a farmer can raise four bushels of wheat with the labor required to raise three without those aids. It is then a matter of entire indifference to him whether you tax him with one-fourth of his crop, or deprive him of the use of the machines. The tax simply deprives him of that additional fourth of his crop which the machine enabled him to raise. The question then takes this shape: What would be the effect on industry of depriving the nation of so much machinery that one-third more labor would be required to produce the same amount of wealth? Here we can appeal to experience. Ten, twenty, or perhaps fifty years ago our people were in this very position. They did not possess our improved machinery, and therefore had to labor one-third more than we do to attain the same result. Was industry then paralyzed? No! They worked harder than we do. They devoted a much larger portion of their labor to articles of prime necessity, and less to the improvement of their minds and the gratification of their tastes.

If, then, our circumstances were changed to correspond to theirs, would not our industry take the same general form that theirs did? Undoubtedly it would. The farmer would raise full as much wheat and the manufacturer spin as much cotton, if one-fourth of his products went for the public benefit, as he now does. Therefore, an enormous tax of this kind is not so ruinous as might at first sight be supposed.

4

As an actual example of the continuance of profitable industry in spite of the taxes, we may cite the prosperity of commerce under import duties of twenty, thirty, or even fifty per cent. Suppose that for a century commerce had been perfectly free, and that it had then been proposed to try the experiment of a duty of only ten per cent. on all imports. We should have heard a universal cry that the measure would be an embargo on all commerce. It would be easily proved that importers did not and could not make ten per cent. profit, and the conclusion would be hastily reached that no one would pay the increased price for imported goods. And it must be admitted that if tried as a temporary experiment, the duties would really be found to produce the predicted evils. At first commerce would be paralyzed and industry disturbed. The importation of some goods might be stopped altogether. Very soon, however, industry would flow into the new and modified channels, people would become accustomed to the new state of things, and no one would be sensible of reaping any less enjoyment from his labor.

Very similar would be the effects of a special war tax, or a return to the imperfect machinery of former times on domestic production. Under any circumstances, it is admitted that a certain length of time, one, two, or perhaps three years would be required for industry to accommodate itself to the new order of things. This change once effected, the tax would not be seriously felt. But the greatest objection of all is found in the fact that if the tax were merely temporary (and being a war tax it would be temporary), industry might not attempt to accommodate itself to the new order of things. To take up once more the illustration by the case of our being obliged to relinquish the use of improved machinery; it cannot be denied that if the deprivation were likely to last but a single year, men would try to eke out their old stock of goods, and get along with the smallest possible amount of new manufactures. The *pro rata* tax on production ought, therefore, to be a permanent one, to be applied to the extinction of the public debt.

How shall this difficulty be avoided? By levying the tax not on production itself, but on the *productive powers*. Levy one-fourth, not of the actual production, but of what the individual is capable of producing. Every man is capable, by the use of his hands or his brains, of earning a certain sum of money annually. Demand from him one-fourth of this sum, leaving him at liberty to earn the other three-fourths or not, as he pleases. There would be required in each congressional district an enrolling officer, whose business it would be to make a register of every male inhabitant above the age of sixteen, capable of employing his faculties so as to benefit the public. Among these individuals the tax would be divided, each man's share being determined by his *profession*, his *in-*

come, and his *wealth*. Regard might also be had to the number of persons dependent on him for support. And in case any one man should not be able to dispose of sufficient of the products of his labor to enable him to pay the tax, the alternative ought to be kept open to him of commuting his tax by working for the Government. Is he a laborer? He can enlist in the army. A farmer? He must sow a larger field of wheat so as to be able to raise his tax money by selling the surplus to the Government. A shoemaker? He must be allowed to make shoes enough for the Government to pay his tax. Thus it will be found that there is not an able-bodied man in the community but can in some way contribute his due share.

The tax on the mercantile portion of the community, using the term mercantile in its largest sense, as including every one who lives by buying and selling at a profit, would be yet more easy. It would best be levied as a percentage, not on profits, but on gross sales. The tax would then include the *income* as well as the per capita tax.

The income tax would be assessed on every producer or manufacturer who earned more than the average amount fixed for his particular profession, and on which the per capita tax was levied.

Finally, we have the tax on capital. Capital gives to its possessor a certain advantage in production which is represented by the rate of interest. Taking the country at large, every man who owns

$100 worth of property can so use that property as to earn from $6 to $8 per year more than he could earn without it. A tax of one-fourth on production would then involve a tax of from 1½ to 2 per cent. on property. As a matter of public policy, however, it is advisable that this source of power should bear a much larger proportion of an *extraordinary expense* like that of war, than mere labor. For in such a case the tax must be apportioned, in a great measure, according to the ability of the payer. Now the capitalist has the same facilities with the man who owns nothing but his hands; and if we taxed him with the entire interest on his capital, he would have left, on the average, as large an income as a man of equal ability would be earning without capital.

Such a system is the alternative of a national debt in carrying on the war. In practice it would not be found so oppressive as might be supposed at first sight, because the Government would, on the average, be a customer buying goods to the same extent that it would be a creditor demanding payment. All the money received from the people would go directly back to the people, and indirectly, in a great measure, to the very persons who contributed it. If the farmer, for example, was required to contribute the value of one-fourth of his crop, either the Government or persons in Government employ would supply him with the required money by buying one-fourth. Thus, practically, the tax would be paid in the form of wheat, cloth, and horses; just what the Government wants.

In arbitrary oppressiveness the system would not be comparable with the Conscription Law, even in the mild form in which we execute the latter. Yet we have seen the latter passed, executed, and approved by the people subject to it without complaint on the score of its oppressiveness. No one has dared to say that a dishonorable peace would be preferable to impressing men into the military service by draft.

As an example of the system proposed, if it is resolved that we shall go on without any further increase of the public debt, on the basis of an annual expenditure of $900,000,000, we may very roughly estimate that the basis of the taxes, and the taxes themselves, would be something like the following:

Able productive males.......................... 4,000,000
Annual product of their labor.................. $3,000,000,000
Valuation of capital........................... 10,000,000,000

The special and extraordinary taxes would be levied each year separately by act of Congress, and would be—

1. Tax on occupation, varying from—say $30 for an unskilled laborer, to $100 or $200 for men of the liberal professions, averaging $50, would yield..... $200,000,000
2. Income tax of 20 per cent. on all who, from superior talents, skill, or fortune, do actually earn more than the minimum on which the first tax is levied.. 70,000,000
3. Property tax of 2½ per cent..................... 250,000,000

The ordinary taxes, to be continued after the close of the war, and applied to the extinction of the public debt already contracted, can easily be increased to.	400,000,000
Making a total revenue, ordinary and extraordinary, of..	920,000,000

We have suggested a large income tax on special classes; but it must be confessed that although in theory such a tax is the most just and equitable that can be assessed, it is in practice the most unequal. It is notorious everywhere in our country, that people enjoying much more than the average amount of wealth, and living in a luxurious style, do still pay an insignificant income tax. This does not always arise from intentional dishonesty. Although the word "income" may in the abstract be susceptible of very exact definition, uncertainty and doubt must continually arise in applying the definition to individual cases. The utmost latitude of interpretation is allowed to every one who does not live on a fixed salary. Hence the taxes ought, whenever possible, to take some other form than this.

The conditions under which a national debt may be advantageous may be seen by comparing the working of the above system with that which we have adopted. The tax-paying community, with respect to occupation, may be divided into three classes:

1. Men whose occupation does not require the use of capital. This class includes laborers, profes-

sional men, Government officers, and all who work for salary, wages, or fees.

2. Men who use capital, whether their own or that of others, and are responsible for its profitable employment, whether they be farmers, manufacturers, or merchants.

3. Men who own capital, but instead of using it themselves loan it to others. Such are owners of shares in all institutions which own money, and all who loan money themselves.

It is singular that we have no words in the English language which accurately designate these three classes of producers. For want of better names they may be called workmen, business men, and capitalists.

The ranks of the third class are naturally recruited from those of the first; and, indeed, the two are to a great extent identical in this country. The workman who loans his money to his employer or puts it into a savings bank, and the professional man who invests his money in bonds of any kind, become capitalists to the extent of their savings. The class of men who live exclusively on the interest of their money is quite small in this country.

Now, when the special war tax is assessed, it may happen that the workman who has not been frugal cannot pay his entire assessment during the year, and cannot enter the Government service without serious inconvenience to his family. It may also happen that the business man is employing his capital so profitably, or that all he has is so necessary to his business that his profits will be materially curtailed by the loss of what he has to pay for carrying on the war. A farmer, for instance, who is assessed $100, may need all the money he can raise for the purchase of agricultural implements and the payment of his laborers. The permission to apply his assessment to this purpose may enable him to raise $10 worth additional of wheat. He may then appeal to a capitalist who can not only pay his own share but the farmer's also, to loan him the money at 6 per cent. interest, and thus make a bargain that shall be mutually advantageous. But the capitalist may not be willing to trust the farmer. Here the Government steps in and borrows the $100 from the capitalist, trusting to gradually obtain principal and interest from the farmer in the form of taxes. This national debt is incurred for the farmer's benefit, who is enabled to lay out $100 more on his farm, on condition of paying the Government the annual interest on that sum.

Herein lies the sole economical advantage of a public debt. It enables that portion of the community which is in the greatest want of capital, to keep possession of what they have, or to add more to it by paying the Government the annual interest on the money they actually owe it. So long as the Government can borrow on such favorable terms that it would be to the advantage of the taxpayers generally to borrow on the same terms, so long is the public debt a public advantage, *and no longer.* The great practical question now is, does our Government borrow money on such terms? Let us see.

A five per cent. bond, interest payable in gold, can now be sold for par in currency; but one dollar of this currency is worth little more than 40 cents in gold, so that we are really paying 12 per cent. interest on the actual amount we borrow. Is it to the advantage of our taxpayers generally to borrow money at 12 per cent. interest? Few, I think, will hold that it is. Then, it cannot tend to the public benefit for our Government to incur any further debt, for in doing so it is, as the agent of the citizens, borrowing money for them on exorbitant terms.

In answer to this there is an argument for preferring indirect taxation extending over a long period, to a large and temporary direct tax, which it is well to consider, granting that it is not for the actual pecuniary interest of the citizen to borrow money on these terms; it is said that the object of the Government is not to raise the money in that way which conduces most to the real welfare of the community, but in such a way as to cause the least amount of complaint. If every man calculated exactly what was for his best interests, these two ways would be identical. But men generally do not make such calculations. Thus, an attendant at church will drop twenty-five cents into the contribution-box every Sunday without any complaint, when he would complain very loudly if obliged to give twelve dollars once a year, although the latter is really more to his advantage than the former. Moreover, the interest on the debt will gradually be paid in taxes which are indirect and insensible, being paid the Government by manufacturers who simply charge them to their customers by increasing the price of their goods. It will thus happen that the owner of a hundred dollar bond will feel richer for possessing it, though obliged to pay indirectly fifteen dollars a year in taxes for interest on his own bond.

To a politician, whose maxim is, "after me the deluge," such an argument as this is very acceptable. But it is unworthy the statesman whose object is the real good of the nation. So long as the entire peace expenses of the Government, including interest on the public debt, can be paid by insensible indirect taxes, it may be well to borrow, even on terms somewhat unfavorable. But we are speedily approaching, if we have not already reached, the point at which insensible indirect taxes will no longer suffice for these objects. When all claims growing out of the war are adjusted, and the entire debt is funded, the annual interest alone will probably amount to $150,000,000, though the rebellion should be suppressed immediately. But in view of the facts that the war for the Union may last much longer, that when it is over we may be engaged in war with a European power, and that a tax on industry heavier than that under which we now labor will discourage emigration, and thus impede the development of our resources, the argument in question invites us to risk our future happiness in order to gratify a present supineness.

It is, indeed, a general and very sound rule, that taxes on production, paid indirectly by the consumer of the articles taxed, are to be preferred to direct taxes, not merely because the consumer does not feel that he is paying a tax, but because he can select his own time of payment. Such rules are very good when the object is to raise a small and definite annual sum in the easiest way; but to apply it to a people in our situation, is as if a man should regulate his exertions to save his house from burning down, by the rules respecting exercise laid down by physiologists.

The increase of the public debt by selling bonds for forty cents on the dollar tends to the unequal distribution of the burdens of war. If principal and interest of the debt is really paid in gold, then the bondholders will be profited at the expense of the taxpayers, who will have to pay just *double* their right share. If they are paid in paper, it will make a complete lottery out of the entire debt, as we shall very clearly see in a subsequent chapter. If they are not paid at all (which God forbid!) the burden of the war will fall entirely on the bondholders. Thus, all is chance where all should be certainty.

If, indeed, the debt were distributed in exact proportion to the taxes to be paid so that every one should pay out in taxes as much as he received in interest, it would cease to be a burden. The idea of such a distribution has already been shown to be chimerical; and if it were possible, there would be need of incurring the debt. For if a man has money to loan the Government, he certainly has money to pay the Government what he owes it. His share of the debt has been incurred solely because it is presumed he has no money to spare.

In fine, let us try to put the matter into a nutshell. Here are twenty millions of people who are, together, to do a certain large and unusual amount of work, in the way of fighting and manufacturing munitions of war.

Under our present system, every one who chooses is allowed, if he escapes conscription, to stay at home and do absolutely nothing to advance the common cause except pay an insignificant indirect tax. Those who really do the work are stimulated thereto by promises to pay, which the Government agrees, at some future time, to make good from the proceeds of taxes which are to be paid by the present do nothing class. Clearly, when these promises have depreciated to forty cents on the dollar, it is time some other system were adopted.

Our true policy is to demand that every man, without exception, shall come forward and do his share of the work. Whenever we organize such a system that this demand is complied with by all, the necessity for borrowing will cease.

Even though the war should end immediately, such a special war tax would be advisable, in order to raise money to pay outstanding claims. The general opinion seems to be that the unadjusted debt amounts to more than five hundred millions; and that if our entire army were disbanded to-morrow, we shall actually find ourselves owing this sum to individuals.

Thus the conclusion seems unavoidable that every consideration of sound policy demands a stop to the further increase of our debt, and the levy of taxes sufficient to meet all the future expenses of the war.

Ought the public debt to be subject to taxation?

There is no reason why the owner of a Government bond should not pay the same tax on it as on any other property of the same kind. The man who loans money to the Government, does not thereby resign either the real ownership or the benefits of the money, for it is all to be returned to him; he ought, therefore, to pay the same taxes on it that he would pay if he kept it for his own use. If he lent his entire property to the Government, when the debt was discharged he would get it all back again without having paid any tax on it at all, unless his bond was taxed.

When the Government sells bonds with a pledge that they shall not be taxed, in order to get more for them, it amounts to selling out, in advance, all the taxes to which the bonds might, in common with other personal property, become subject. This "farming out" of taxes to be collected, for this is what the contract amounts to, is the worst possible way of borrowing money. It was an accompaniment, partly cause and partly effect, of that miserable condition of the finances of France which preceded the first revolution. If, then, it has proved disadvantageous when the amount of the tax is known beforehand, how much more so in the present case, when no one can know how heavy a property tax the Government may have to levy? The increased price obtained for the bonds is probably quite small, perhaps insignificant; yet, if the Government should think proper to levy a property tax of five per cent. it would lose $100,000,000 by being obliged to remit the tax on the present public debt. It is, therefore, to be hoped that in the sales of bonds to be hereafter authorized, the Government will bind itself only to levy no higher taxes on them than on other personal property.

CHAPTER IV.

THE LEGAL TENDER NOTES—THEIR INFLUENCE ON PUBLIC CREDIT.

DURING the third session of the thirty-seventh Congress, in the winter of 1861-'2, the financial situation of the Government, on a superficial view, presented many inauspicious features. To the public mind the future was all doubt and uncertainty. A war of unknown duration, with expenditures of unheard of magnitude, were in prospect. We had but a faint idea of our capacity for sustaining a long war. Forty millions of demand notes were in circulation, and payment would be due whenever the holders chose to ask for it. A much larger debt, in the form of interest-bearing treasury notes, would be due at various intervals during the next three years. During the same period the debt would be increased many fold by the vast war expenditures. There was no prospect that the money required by the Government could be borrowed on favorable terms, and a system of taxation was hardly thought of. The State banks, through which the war loans had hitherto been negotiated, could supply no more money. Six per cent. stock, which, in prosperous times, would command a heavy premium, was at a discount of from seven to fifteen per cent. Its price would probably fall lower yet; how much lower no one could divine.

Matters were made worse by the general suspension of specie payments by the banks at the end of 1861. There would be a general flow of the demand notes to the Treasury for redemption. To prevent this flow the Treasury ignobly followed the example of the banks, by refusing to redeem the notes.

February 25, 1862, an act was passed authorizing the issue of certain United States notes. The provisions of this act are too well known to require any statement of them. There has, indeed, been some difference of opinion whether the notes thus authorized ought to be called "paper money," and spoken of as "irredeemable;" but this is purely a question of terminology. Webster defines paper money as "Notes or bills issued by authority and promising the payment of money, circulated as the representative of coin." In mercantile language a bill is said to be "redeemable" when the drawer is ready to pay it. It is notorious that the bills in question answered to the above definition, and that the Treasury was not ready then, and is not ready yet, to pay them. Therefore, to take the ground that they were neither "paper money" nor "irredeemable" is not to defend them, but to attack the definitions of Webster, and the common forms of speech used by the business world.

It is proposed to examine the notes thus authorized from three distinct standpoints.

In the present chapter attention will be called to the principles involved in the measure, and the effect on the public credit of the adoption of such principles.

Next, we shall examine into the effects on the business and other interests of the country.

Finally, to judge whether the system devised was really the best one, we shall inquire how far the notes were expedient and necessary; compare them with previous systems of paper currency, such as our Continental money, and the assignats of the French revolution; and examine the arguments urged in their favor.

The object of the measure was two fold: it was intended to alleviate the burden of the debt already contracted, and to pay certain of the future expenses of the war. First let us see how the former object was attained. There were notes in circulation, issued by authority of Congress, to the amount of some $35,000,000 each bearing the words "THE UNITED STATES WILL PAY THE BEARER —— DOLLARS ON DEMAND." The United States had not, at the moment, the necessary number of dollars to pay with. So the "bearers" were met and checkmated by a timely *revision of the Dictionary.*

If men had examined the acts of Congress with a view of learning exactly what was the legal meaning of the word "dollars" in the promise "will pay the bearer —— dollars," he would have found it to be as follows:

DOLLAR. A coin of the United States containing $23\frac{2}{10}$ grains of fine gold.

These thirty five millions of dollars, therefore, meant more than eight hundred million grains of gold. Could not the meaning of the word "dollar" be so altered as to include something more easily commanded than gold? Without discussing the legal question whether it *could* be so altered or not, the historical fact is that it *was* so altered. It was made to read:

DOLLAR. A piece of paper stamped "United States will pay one dollar.—Legal tender for one dollar:" etc.

Since these pieces of paper could be commanded at a very small cost, it is obvious that there was a great saving and a great relief at least for the time being. As soon as the plates could be engraved, and the printing presses be put in successful operation, the Treasury was prepared to fulfil the promise, "United States will pay the bearer —— dollars." So whenever the holder of a demand note thereafter presented it at the Treasury and persisted in demanding payment, he received another note, with the words "on demand" left off, and the debt was for the time being discharged.

It was not the demand notes alone that were thus provided for. The new paper money was a legal tender in payment of the entire *principal* of the public debt. How would this operate? In the course of the preceding twelve months, when twenty millions of hearts were all aglow with enthusiasm for their flag and their country, thousands of old stockings in every State had poured their golden contents into the treasury of the nation. Thousands of mechanics, farmers, and workmen, each gave a hard-earned hundred of gold dollars to support the credit of the Government. They received in return $7\frac{3}{10}$ notes; promises that the United States would repay them the "dollars" in three years. The new definition of dollar was applied to the entire principal of these notes also. It was enacted that when the holder of the 7-30 note presented it at the Treasury for payment, instead of getting his gold dollars back, he should be paid in dollars which were obtained by the Government at the cost of paper and printing unless he preferred a six per cent. bond. The promise to pay would be legally cancelled by the delivery of another promise to pay.

Now let us consider an ethical question. Why might not Congress have enacted as follows:

That the notes known as seven-thirties shall, after they become due, be a legal tender for all debts public and private, when so stamped at the Treasury?

Then, when the holder of the note presented it for payment, the teller would simply stamp it "Legal Tender," and hand it back, and the debt would be paid. Would it not have been just as satisfactory to the creditor to be paid in this way as to be paid in a new note? It certainly would. The old note stamped would have been legal tender equally with the new one; and it was just as easy as not to give it all the elements of value of the new note by receiving it in payment of debts and loans.

In fact, a law was actually passed which permitted the demand notes to be redeemed in this way. They also were declared a legal tender in payment of debts. Consequently, when the bearer of the note presented it for payment, the teller could pay it by handing back either the identical note presented, or another one exactly like it, without even the trouble of stamping. Quite likely this formality was not actually gone through with in a single case; more especially as the old demand notes, being receivable for customs, were more valuable than the new ones in which the teller would have been equally at liberty to redeem them. Consequently, it would have been to the positive injury of the note holder to allow the Government to redeem its promise in the altered way.

This ethical question gives rise to a few others. They are not asked in a spirit of censoriousness, nor with the idea of intimating that there can be but one answer to them; but simply to induce the reader to study the subject from an ethical point of view. Was the operation we have described—that of paying one note with another—paying the debt expressed by the first note? If so, was it paying the debt in the manner understood between the parties at the time the debt was contracted? If not, what is the "dishonored public faith" and "national bankruptcy" of which Mr. Chase so emphatically warned Congress not three months before?

No elaborate argument can be necessary to make it obvious to any unprejudiced mind, that such measures as have been described could not be otherwise than most injurious to the credit of the Government. That promises made by the Government were modified without the consent of the party in whose favor they were made, is undeniable. The promise meant one thing at the time it was made; the meaning of the words was afterwards changed so that it should mean something else. Gold had been the only legal tender of the Government since the adoption of the Constitution. For the first hundred million of the 7–30 notes it would accept nothing but gold, or its absolute equivalent. Among those who thus loaned the metal gold to the Government, no one for a moment supposed that if the loan were ever repaid at all, it would be repaid in any thing but gold.

It would be entirely useless to inquire whether the measure in question was a breach of public faith. If every citizen of the country, and every holder of bonds, were to believe and maintain that the act was perfectly right, it would not prevent the evil effects in the least, but only exaggerate them. The relation of cause and effect is as invariable in the world of mind as it is in the world of matter. We need not decide whether a moral cause is right or wrong in order to trace it to its consequences. If the effects of the legal tender notes depended on the purity of the motives of our statesmen in issuing them, they would undoubtedly be good. But such is not the case. In so far as the effects are bad, the adoption of the measure was like setting fire to a wooden house. The house will burn down equally whether the act of setting it on fire was right or wrong, necessary or unnecessary.

On the very same principles Great Britain could relieve herself of the burden of her entire public debt in a single month by ordering an issue to the public creditors of legal tender notes for the debt as fast as it became payable. Perhaps if we cannot see the beam in our own eye, we may nevertheless see the mote in our neighbor's eye, and divine the effect of such a measure on the public credit of the British Empire, whether the measure itself should be necessary or unnecessary. Indeed a Government could in the very same way make its contracts mean any thing it pleased by altering the legal meaning of the words which entered into them.

In our own case the change would have been less to the disadvantage of the bondholder, had any efficient measures been taken to give the legal tender money a definite gold value. It may be replied that three measures were taken to this end:

1. The notes were declared lawful money and legal tender.

2. They were redeemable, not directly in coin, but in the class of securities familiarly known as "five-twenty bonds."

3. They are themselves part of the public debt, inasmuch as each note contains a promise that the United States will pay the bearer the amount of its face.

Perhaps it is hardly necessary to argue the first point. No Government was ever powerful enough to compel its paper money to be considered as the equivalent of coin, for this would be to control the most secret thoughts and opinions of men. Whatever might have been thought of the case in the beginning, few will now pretend that our paper dollars are in any way the equivalent of the gold dollars which could be legally demanded for every debt previous to Feb. 25, 1862. Let us look at the question in a general light. Why should a note stamped by authority of the Government "Legal tender for one dollar," be worth twenty-three grains of gold rather than five grains or one grain? Why should it be worth our gold dollar rather than a German thaler? I can see no reason. Making the notes legal tender adds nothing to their value. You can, indeed, pay off an old debt with them as with gold, because the creditor cannot help himself; but when you come to buy flour and butter, you find the holders graduate their prices to correspond to the new value of the dollar. You find that although Congress can declare notes legal tender, it cannot fix the price of provisions.

2. The legal tender notes now issued are not redeemable in five-twenties or any other specified form of security. They are, indeed, receivable for all loans; but as the loans can be negotiated only on such terms as the Government chooses to accede to, this adds nothing to the value of the notes. The first issue of notes was redeemable in the bonds alluded to. Hence their value could not fall below that of the bonds, for which they could at any time be exchanged. But how was the value of the bonds fixed? By the terms of the legal tender act the Government could redeem the bonds at any time after five years in legal tender notes. The value of the bonds was therefore fixed by the value of the future legal tender notes, which might be much less than that of the present ones. There was no promise or pledge, expressed or implied, that the money with which the principal should be discharged should have any intrinsic value whatever. There was, indeed, no doubt that it would be discharged in something which would be declared lawful money by Act of Congress; but what one hun-

dred dollars of this money, when received, would be worth, no man in the country knew then; no man in the country knows now. They may be paid in gold, in lawful money the equivalent of gold, or in lawful money one thousand dollars of which will not buy a barrel of flour, without any breach of promise on the part of the Government.

Had the faith of the nation been unequivocably pledged that both principal and interest of the new bonds should be paid in coin of the same weight and standard as that already authorized by law; had the national legislature likewise declared, that the sense of the country demanded that every obligation into which the Government had previously entered should be discharged exactly as was understood at the time of entering; had they in consequence provided for the payment of the demand notes and the "seven-thirties" in coin, the former immediately, the latter at maturity; then, I can scarcely conceive that the bonds in question could have fallen very much below gold. But whether this idea is correct or not, whether the measures proposed would or would not have given a great impulse to public credit, it is certain that, as the case stood, no definite value could be assigned to the money in which the principal of the bonds might be paid. Making notes redeemable in bonds which were again redeemable in notes, was like trying to keep a ship from blowing to sea by lashing her to another, and then anchoring this one by lashing her to the first.

The *interest* of the public debt was excepted from the operation of the legal tender act. This was the great redeeming feature of the bill. But for it, our currency might now be rapidly following our Continental money, and the present currency of the rebels, in the road to ruin. But a great part of the good effect which might have resulted from this proviso, was lost from the circumstance that there was no pledge of faith to continue paying the interest in coin for any specified length of time. The bill simply enacted that the notes should be lawful money, and a legal tender in payment of all debts except duties on imports and interest on the public debt, which should be paid in coin. There would certainly have been no greater breach of faith in including the interest of the debt in the operation of the law than in including the principal; and if one Congress can declare paper a legal tender for one debt, the next Congress can declare it legal tender for another. At the same time every enlightened friend of the credit of the country cannot but earnestly hope that the interest on the present funded debt will never be paid in anything but coin of the present standard.

3. The legal tender notes are, indeed, counted as part of the public debt, but the time when this debt is to be paid is entirely unknown. Equally unknown is the kind or value of the money in which it is to be paid. If it is not to be paid for a century its present value as a debt is very inconsiderable.

Indeed, so long as the present law is in force, every note would seem to be virtually legal tender for its own payment. Whenever it is presented at the Treasury, it can be legally redeemed in another note just like it, and this second note can be redeemed by returning the first. So the note has not necessarily any value at all as a Government debt.

It is, then, quite plain that there was no necessary limit to the possible depreciation of the new notes. But the circumstance that a fixed gold value was not given to the notes, is not of itself the great evil to be complained of.

We may say of every act of a Government or an individual, that it involves and is founded on some principle, and some general rule of conduct. In many cases the principles involved in the act are really of much more importance than the act itself, because they may be the occasion of a long series of analogous acts. If a trader makes false representations in the sale of goods, the *general* fact that he cannot be trusted is of far greater importance than the particular fact that on such a day he cheated you. The evil of an unjust imprisonment is not that Mr. A or Mr. B has been deprived of liberty for a few hours, but that a principle has been established under the operation of which personal liberty is no longer secure.

So with the measures under consideration; their real evil lay, not in the inception of a fact, but in the establishment of a principle. It was not that we declared paper a legal tender, but that we adopted a rule of action under the operation of which public credit was but an empty sound. It was not that the Treasury happened to be in a strait for money, but that it pretended to pay when it did not. The fact that the measure was accepted by the country as a just and proper one made the matter worse, because the sanction of public opinion was thus given to a ruinous principle, and the principle was, for this reason, more likely to become a standard policy. On the other hand, the more unfavorable the light in which the public view the measure; the more they reprobate the principles involved in it; and the less they are disposed to justify them or accept them as the basis of a permanent policy, the better. For the credit of a people will always correspond to their standard of public honesty as indicated by their acts and opinions. Consequently, whenever the nation clearly sees that measures injurious to the public credit are fundamentally wrong, and manifests a desire to repudiate or modify them at the earliest moment, its credit will by the general recognition of that state of feeling be restored. The nation as a seeker of credit is in the position of an individual, against whom payment can be enforced by no law except his own sense of justice. It is more important that his sense of justice shall be correct and delicate, than that he shall have ready money.

The legal tender notes naturally grew out of the

suspension of specie payments by the treasury two months before. Considering only the present exigencies of the Government, the views which our people had been accustomed to entertain respecting the extent of the obligation to pay a circulating note, and the general practice of the banks throughout the country, this act was a comparatively harmless, and very necessary one. But let us measure it by that high standard of faith which ought to be adopted by the statesman who desires to see his generation bequeath an untarnished honor to posterity.

Let us see how it would be with individuals placed in circumstances similar to those of the Government, in the first part of 1862. A creditor holds notes against such a person. He demands payment, and the following conversation ensues:

Debtor. Cannot pay it. I have not money enough to pay all notes of that kind, so to be impartial I shall not pay any. The banks have suspended, and so have I.

Creditor. When can you pay it?

Debtor. Don't know: cannot answer any more questions.

This was no doubt the substance of the conversation between the teller and every one who presented a note at the Treasury between the suspension of specie payments and the issue of the legal tender notes. Not only the obligation to pay on demand, but, so far as the public could discern, all obligation to pay at all until the holder should chance to owe an equal debt to the Government, was deliberately repudiated. This weak, timeserving, and timid act is a principal link in the chain which has brought on all our subsequent difficulties. No man who believes that honesty is the best policy, that a nation as well as an individual in search of credit, should exhibit the most scrupulous honor in fulfilling all obligations, can doubt that the counsels which suggested this course were the very worst that could be adopted. It was a critical period in our financial history. Fear and confidence fought for the mastery in the minds of the community. Had the Treasury allied itself with the side of confidence by resolutely continuing specie payments, it might have prevailed. The suspension, except during the short time necessary to negotiate a temporary loan, was as unnecessary and unjustifiable as it was weak. A heavy tax, say six per cent. per annum, on the repudiated bank circulation, would of itself have stopped the run on the Treasury in forty-eight hours after it was imposed. The banks would then have called in their notes as rapidly as possible, and there would have been a positive necessity for either gold, demand notes, or other Government money to fill the vacuum. No doubt such a measure would have seemed harsh and ungrateful, and would have caused much complaint on the part of the banks. But, which is of most importance, the honor of the Government and the moral stamina of the nation, or the interest of those corporations? It must be remembered that such a tax would only have deprived the banks of a source of profit to which the Government has a far better right than they; namely, the interest on the money circulating through the channels of business. Indeed, as we shall see in the next chapter, the course actually pursued has been far more disastrous to the bank interests than would have been a compulsory prohibition of all their business.

It may not be uninteresting to examine more fully that state of public sentiment which led the nation to look with so little dissatisfaction upon the act in question.

The general complacence with which our mercantile community look upon the failure of a house to make good its obligations, the frequency of such failures, and the circumstance that they are not looked upon as compromising the honor of the defaulters in any degree whatever, have been thrown into our faces by our transatlantic brethren as indicative of our very lax notions of public morality. The imputation is neither just nor reasonable, so long as good faith is kept between the parties. When one merchant gives credit to another, or furnishes a young man with a stock in trade, it is done with the tacit understanding that the obligation of the debtor ceases, if, through losses in business, he becomes unable to pay. The creditor of course charges a little more on account of the risk; he insures the debt as an insurance company would insure a house, and it may be that this system of debt insurance is as beneficial to the community as fire insurance. It certainly is as honest.

But when we extend this system of debt insurance into transactions of a public character we start on the road to infinite evil. The frequency with which our banks have for a longer or shorter period suspended specie payments has habituated the public to read every bank note with the mental reservation "if we do not suspend," just as every promissory note contained the understood proviso "if I am able." Now, the question arises, *ought this, or any other proviso to be understood as qualifying the promises to pay of our Government?* Most certainly not, except as circumstances absolutely beyond the control of the Treasury might temporarily compel it. Absolute inability of the nation to redeem its obligations to its own citizens is almost a physical impossibility. For, as has been shown in the last chapter, paying such a debt is nothing more than equalizing the unequal contributions of individual citizens, so that each one shall have contributed his just share.

The evils of the Treasury suspension were greater than those involved in the suspension of the banks, owing to the different conditions of the two institutions. A well-managed bank always holds in its vaults either coin or promissory notes of responsible individuals sufficient to pay all demands upon it, and to make good its capital beside. All these notes would be due in less than ninety and perhaps less than sixty days, depending on the length of time of discount. The Government, on the other hand, held no such notes, and payment would have to be left entirely to its sense of good faith. Hence the more disastrous consequences of its refusal to pay as promised. But the Government had a power which the banks had not, that of levying taxes to any extent on the whole country, so that its failure could be due only to its own supineness.

But failing to see any more serious consequences in the Treasury suspension than in the bank suspensions, the nation supinely submitted to it, as something which could not be helped, and which did not involve any degradation of the public faith. The credit of the banks had not generally been impaired by their suspension, or by the general expectation of such an act. Why should that of the Government? So, notwithstanding the fear of the people exhibited by the Treasury, and notwithstanding the vote of want of confidence in the nation implied in the legal tender bill, which two months after the suspension protected the Treasury against the assaults of its creditors by surrounding it with a parapet of legal tender paper, the confidence of the nation was not at first impaired. This is conclusively proved by the gold value of the National bonds. The twenty-year sixes, a month after the passage of the act, brought 96 in gold, showing conclusively that the people had no idea that the principles involved in the recent acts would be carried out to their legitimate conclusion. The evils of a redundant currency had just been so clearly depicted by the Honorable Secretary of the Treasury, and the general determination to sustain the credit of the nation was so strong, that every one felt confident that efficient measures would be taken to guard the currency against serious depreciation. Had any one predicted that in three years the notes which were declared a legal tender for the entire principal of the public debt, would only have been worth from 40 to 45 cents on the dollar in gold, he would have been looked upon as a villanous slanderer of the public credit.

Yet their history exhibits the same characteristics which have been exhibited by every system of paper money not redeemable in coin. The magic word "dollar" had at first a great influence over the minds of the community. *Value* being something which could not be seen, felt, or heard, but only learned from the exhibition of public demand in the market, it was thought that any thing declared a dollar by act of Congress must be as valuable as any thing which had formerly been declared a dollar. But, as additional issues of legal tender paper began to be emitted or called for, as these issues began to be recommended on the miserable plea of their necessity, as men began to see that this paper money had absolutely no fixed basis of value whatever, and that there was no apparent disposition on the part of the Government to form any such basis for it; then the prices of things began to rise, and gold to rise with them.

The actual cause of public credit, as a matter of fact, not of theory, as it existed in the minds of the community, not in the speeches of politicians, is shown by the following table. This shows for each month—1. The average price of gold in legal tender notes; 2. The value in gold of $100 in legal tender notes; 3. The market value in gold of 6 per cent. bonds, accrued interest for the half year taken off.

		Price of Gold.	Gold value of $100 in legal tender notes.	Gold value of $100 20-years 6 per cent. bond.
1862.	March	1.02	98	90
	April	1.02	98	91
	May	1.03	97	99
	June	1.06	94	98
	July	1.16	86	86
	August	1.15	87	87
	September	1.19	84	84
	October	1.30	77	79
	November	1.31	76	78
	December	1.32	76	76
1863.	January	1.44	70	67
	February	1.61	62	60
	March	1.51	66	67
	April	1.51	66	68
	May	1.48	68	72
	June	1.46	69	73
	July	1.31	76	80
	August	1.26	79	83
	September	1.33	75	79
	October	1.46	69	74
	November	1.47	68	73
	December	1.52	66	70

		Price of Gold.	Gold value of $100 in legal tender notes.	Gold value of $100 20-years 6 per cent. bond.
1864	January	1.54	65	69
	February	1.60	63	69
	March	1.64	61	67
	April	1.75	57	61
	May	1.80	56	62
	June	1.95	51	54
	July	2.50	40	42
	August	2.56	39	41
	September	2.28	44	47
	October	2.06	49	51
	November	2.24	45	48
	December	2.30	44	48

The two last columns of this table, which show the actual gold value at which the Government notes and bonds have been held, is worthy of very serious attention. Whatever metaphysical themes may be propounded about the demonetization of gold, and its conversion into an article of merchandise, the following three facts are thoroughly understood by the mercantile community:

1. Gold and silver have for centuries been the standard of *value* in every civilized country.

2. Gold now is the standard of value in our own as in every other civilized country, in spite of the legal tender paper.

3. Gold will be the standard of value in this and every other civilized country, in spite of any thing any Government may do to prevent it.*

---

* The fact that prices in general do not fluctuate in exact correspondence with gold, no more disproves these general propositions than the existence of mountains disproves the rotundity of the earth.

These unchangeable facts being taken for granted, does the circumstance that our six per cent. bonds, in the public market, will only bring fifty cents on the dollar in coin, imply any doubt of the Government faith? This depends, in part, on what standard of credit the Government is supposed to adopt. If legal tender notes are to be the permanent Government currency, its credit in this respect is very good; indeed all that can be desired, and more than could be expected, showing most conclusively that the people look forward to some better standard than that. If the bonds are to be considered as redeemable in paper, it is as absurd to measure them by a gold standard as it would be to assume that a dollar meant a pound sterling. In fact, in the case supposed it is impossible to fix any gold value for the bonds, because no one can predict the gold value of future legal tender notes. It is as if you held a note against an individual for 100 piastres, when neither he nor you knew how much a piastre was; when no one knew, in fact, because its value would have to be fixed by future legislation. In such a case your unwillingness to consider the piastre as the equivalent of the gold dollar would not involve any doubt of the good faith of the drawer of the note.

But, if both principal and interest of the debt are to be paid in gold coin, our public credit is practically not good. In ordinary times five per cent. bonds are worth par in our markets. True, the effect of the war has been to increase the rate of profit on capital for the time being; but this increase is only temporary, so that a seven or eight per cent. bond, if it has many years to run, ought to be worth par, and probably would be if its security were perfect. Since, then, our six per cent. bonds are only worth about 50 in gold; since, in order to borrow the equivalent of $100 in coin, we must not only pay $12 per annum interest, but $200 for principal at maturity, it must be conceded that the community does not feel universally assured of receiving both principal and interest of those bonds in gold coin of the present standard. If any additional proof of this fact is wanting, it is found in the much higher price commanded by Massachusetts bonds of similar character. Why are Massachusetts bonds preferred to those of the United States? Let our consciences answer this question for us.

While it can hardly be controverted that the low gold price of our bonds does imply some doubt of their being paid in gold, we cannot measure this doubt by the amount of the depreciation. The latter depends in part on certain attributes of human nature. No man will give any thing for a debt not payable until twenty years have elapsed, unless he takes an interest in his future self. Now, although to a certain extent most civilized men are disposed to provide for the far future as carefully as for the present, this disposition speedily finds a limit. They are quite willing to invest their ordinary surplus earnings for the benefit of the future. But when it comes to making those unusual exertions necessary in the prosecution of a great war, the prospect of future pecuniary benefit speedily loses part of its hold on the mind. Men will want larger and larger promises to stimulate them to the same exertions, no matter how certain of fulfilment those promises may be. Thus a great depreciation of any kind of bonds is the necessary result of throwing more of them on the market than will absorb the ordinary surplus earnings of that class of the community who consider them perfectly secure. The more frugal this class, that is, the more willing they are to labor and exercise self-denial for a future good, the less will be the depreciation from overloading the market.

But apart from all questions of frugality among the people and right principles on the part of the Government, a diminution of the gold value of bonds is the necessary result of an issue of notes in payment of indebtedness. Respecting the manner in which the Government will discharge its debts, we have all shades of opinion. Many are fully convinced that its every promise will be redeemed in coin, and would be willing to give par in gold for six per cent. bonds if they could not get them any cheaper. Now let us see how paying in paper has operated on this class. Let us take, for instance, the $7\frac{3}{10}$ notes, issued in 1861. There are, we will suppose, five persons of equal wealth, each of whom would have paid $100, had this loan been assessed as a tax. But one of them, being a firm and confident believer in the Government, paid the share of all five, by loaning the Government $500 for three years, thereby rendering the tax, for the time being, unnecessary. If, now, at the end of three years, the Government determines to pay off this debt in coin, it simply levies a direct tax equal to the entire amount of the loan, receiving the $7_{\frac{3}{10}}$ notes in payment therefor. The confident man will now get $400 of his gold back again, either by his four neighbors each coming to buy $100 of his loan in order to pay their tax, or by the Government paying his notes in gold. The debt will then be discharged by the equitable division of its burdens among all, as it ought to be. The confident man, having got his gold back, and found his faith in the Government vindicated, will be willing to loan the gold to the Government again on favorable-terms, and the gold value of bonds will be as great as ever.

But by failing to levy this tax, and compelling the creditor to fund his debt, *we place it out of his power to make another loan to the Government,* no matter how little his good opinion of the public faith may have been shocked by the failure to compel an equitable division of the war expense. The Government is, therefore, compelled to borrow from those who have less faith in it and less disposition to invest money for the future. Thus the measure under consideration necessarily paralyzes the efforts of those who have faith in the Government, and compels it to resort for further loans to those who doubt whether it will make good its promises.

Is it not a short-sighted policy which has thus punished our friends, and played into the hands of our enemies?

A system of paper money may be described, in general, as *a convenient device for throwing the entire burden of an extraordinary expense upon that class of the community who have most faith in the paper money.* Such a system necessarily acts in this way. It was so in the revolutionary war. The tory, who had no faith in the redemption of the money, always parted with what he received as soon as possible, by purchasing the necessaries of life from the more confident patriots. As the currency depreciated prices rose, and the tories, having thus got a large portion of the army supplies in their own possession, charged their own price for them. Thus the patriots and the cause lost, and the tories gained. The first bore the entire burden, the last none.

The uncertainty which hangs over the real value of the future "dollar" is much to be deplored. At present a simple promise on the part of the Government to pay $119 in three years, being principal and interest of a three years' compound interest note, will only bring 45 cents in gold in the public market. Why is this? Simply because no living man can judge what will be the value of those dollars when he gets them. The holder of the note may be paid in gold or its equivalent. In that case he will have made an enormous profit by keeping possession of the note. On the other hand, he may be paid in paper, one hundred dollars of which will not buy ten in gold, without any breach of faith on the part of the Government. Every thing depends on the relation between the public expenditures and the receipts from loans and taxes. Should our receipts be greater than our expenditures, and the volume of the currency begin to diminish in consequence, the value of the dollar must rise rapidly. Should the war and our present financial policy both be continued, no one can tell how little a paper dollar may be worth.

How is the principal of the *funded* public debt, the five-twenties, for example, to be paid? This question is intimately connected with the value of the future dollar, and we have already shown that the present state of our credit depends very much on the answer to it. Here the Government is a great loser, merely from the uncertainty which hangs over the question. By the letter and spirit of the legal tender act the bonds can be redeemed in notes at any time after five years. We tacitly repudiated all obligation to pay any portion of the principal of the public debt in coin, and lenders took us at our word by giving us no more for them than for bonds payable in paper. This was perfectly natural, because it was not to be supposed that we would deal any better by the public creditors than we were bound to by the terms of the contract. But about the time the five-twenty loan was all taken, an official announcement was issued from the Treasury that the principal of the entire permanent debt should be paid in coin. Thus we are placed in the following dilemma: If we pay the principal in coin, we shall give the creditors much more than they are entitled to by the strict terms of the contract. If we pay in paper, we shall be accused of a breach of faith by foreigners who bought bonds without being aware of the terms of the act authorizing their issue.

Every enlightened lover of our country's good name should be gratified that the loan of 1841, due January 1, 1863, was paid in coin. But the reasons assigned for this act are such as must have annulled whatever good effect it might otherwise have produced. They are found in communications from the Presidents of the principal New York City banks, and from the Honorable Secretary of the Treasury, laid before the House of Representatives January 6, 1863. Had Congress been emphatically assured that every instinct of good faith and manly honesty demanded that this loan should be paid in coin, because coin was the only lawful money when the loan was contracted, and that such a degradation of the national honor as would be involved in the discharge of the loan in paper would consign the authors of the act to the just execration of enlightened posterity; and, had this view of the case been accepted by the nation, our credit would have been placed on a firm basis. Instead of such views as this, we find that the act of paying in coin is apologized for on the ground of its expediency. The bankers advise the Honorable Secretary that the credit of the Government at home and abroad would be greatly promoted by payment in coin, while a failure to meet the just expectations of the public and the holders of the loan, in this respect, would deteriorate the value of all government stocks to an extent far exceeding the whole sum in question (about $3,000,000). The Secretary adds that his judgment " was determined in favor of coin, not merely by the weighty considerations growing out of its beneficial influences on public credit," but by the circumstance that the needed specie could be obtained with great ease. It was, in fact, loaned by the banks at four per cent. interest.

That these reasons do not suffice to place the credit of the nation on the required footing will be evident on reflecting that we want, not a reason founded on temporary and adventitious circumstances, but a *universal rule of conduct;* a rule founded on such reasons that it *cannot be departed from.* We want an authoritative and unequivocal recognition by Congress and the country of this principle. *Good faith demands that every loan contracted by the Government when coin only was a legal tender should be paid in coin.*

The rule finally laid down by Mr. Chase, and already referred to in speaking of the principal of the five-twenties was, that the principal of the permanent debt, including all bonds, should be paid in coin, but that the principal of all the temporary loan was payable in legal tender notes. This decision gives rise to the ethical question, How does the circumstance that a loan is "temporary" modify the obligation to pay it? The difficulty of answering it is increased by the circumstance that the five-twenty loan, declared payable in *coin*, was all contracted by borrowing *paper*, while the seven-thirty loan, declared payable in *paper*, was nearly all contracted by borrowing *coin*.

It has sometimes been urged, in extenuation of the act of refusing to pay the latter loan in coin, that there was no agreement to pay it thus. If we admit such a plea as this, our credit is good for nothing. See what courses the plea would justify: Congress has enacted that a number of debts and dues should be paid in coin, but has never agreed to pay any thing in *gold* coin. So a special coinage of bronze dollars of the same weight as the gold dollar might be authorized, and the entire interest of the public debt might be paid in this worthless bronze, merely because the word "gold" did not appear before the word "coin." And even, should gold coin be distinctly named in the agreement, the quantity of pure gold in the dollar might be indefinitely reduced on the plea that Congress had never agreed to continue the same weight of gold in the dollar. It is clear that a people who would swindle by such verbal quibbles would neither deserve nor enjoy any credit whatever.

It has already been argued that a further increase of the public debt is neither necessary nor expedient. But, if borrow we must, our true course is to negotiate all future loans on a gold basis, by borrowing nothing but gold coin or bullion, and agreeing to pay nothing but a given weight of *gold coin*. This coin may then be sold for currency at the highest market rates. At the present price of gold every million in coin would cancel $2\frac{1}{4}$ millions of the public debt, and diminish the volume of the currency by the same amount. Government would receive proposals, not for a purchase of bonds, but for a loan of bullion (or coin), repayable at the pleasure of the Government after one, three, or five years, and holders would be asked simply to specify the lowest rate of interest which they would accept. It would be better for the Government to pay twelve, or even fifteen per cent. interest on such a loan, than to sell 10-40 bonds at par. Borrowing a million, for example, at fourteen per cent. interest, the principal and interest will be as follows:

    Principal, ... $1,000,000
    Annual interest, . .   140,000

At the present price of gold (January, 1865) Government will receive $2,300,000 in currency for the million in coin. To command the same amount of currency by the sale of 10-40 bonds, the debt would be—

Principal, ...	$2,300,000
Annual interest, . .	115,000

Thus, while borrowing bullion at fourteen per cent., the interest would be greater by $25,000, the principal would be less by more than half. Does the country really comprehend that for every $100 received into the treasury from loans, we not only pay $12 interest, but agree to pay $230 for principal? While we cannot cancel the present debt without paying $130 premium on every hundred borrowed, we can cancel that proposed without paying any premium, whenever the Government is able to borrow money at less than fourteen per cent. interest.

It may be asked, "Why have a double transfer of gold? If we can get par in gold for the bonds, we can get the equivalent of gold in currency. Then why not sell the bonds directly for currency, and thus save handling the gold?"

There are two reasons why the bonds should be negotiated only for gold, or its absolute equivalent: The true state of the public credit will then be evident to the country, and, if it is bad, means will undoubtedly be taken to improve it. An evil must be seen and felt before any great pains will be taken to heal it. The present system of receiving legal tender notes as *gold* in exchange for gold bonds, and paying them out as paper, supplies a convenient hole, in which, ostrich like, to hide our heads to the true state of our credit. Doubtless great numbers of loyal citizens think that so long as a 10-40 bond will bring par in legal tender notes the Government credit is good. This is as if an importer should think he was making a profit so long as he sold his goods for a higher price in paper than he paid in gold.

The great reason for borrowing bullion is, that there would be no doubt how the debt should be paid. That unfortunate and much abused word "Dollar," the meaning of which can be fixed by any subsequent Congress to suit the real or supposed exigencies of the times, ought not to be suffered to appear in the contract. The bond should be a pledge of faith to pay a certain specified *weight* of gold coin or bullion. The advantage of such a contract will appear from the consideration that the depreciation of the gold value of our bonds may be traced to three sources:

1. Throwing such large quantities on the market.

2. Fear on the part of the community that something may happen to the Government to cause a general destruction of the national debt.

3. Fear that the word "dollar," or "dollar in coin," may, 10 or 30 years hence, mean something different from what it does now.

Now, it is plain that, while the first two causes would not be avoided by the proposed plan, the last would. It is, therefore, worth trying, at the least.

CHAPTER V.

INFLUENCE OF THE LEGAL TENDER NOTES ON PRIVATE FAITH AND THE BUSINESS OF THE COUNTRY.

The value of the entire circulating medium of a country, be it gold, silver, paper, or wampum, is subject to this general law: that it can never be increased beyond a certain limit, no matter how much you may increase the volume of currency. The total value of the money actually required to transact the business of the United States is, on an average, about $250,000,000 in gold. When business is "brisk," and a great deal of buying and selling is done, the value of the money increases; when business is dull it diminishes. Thus it may, under certain circumstances, rise to $300,000,000, or fall to $200,000,000. A paper issue, though irredeemable, will not depreciate materially so long as its amount is kept within the required limit; but, exceed this limit, and depreciation is inevitable. If the amount is double what is necessary, it will depreciate to one half; if treble, to one third, and so on. But we must consider as currency proper only that portion of the money of the community which is actually in use for the purpose of buying goods or paying debts. If any is hoarded, either for its own sake or for the purpose of finally putting it to some other use than buying, it must be excluded from our estimate of the total value. Hence gold and silver must be excluded whenever they have ceased to circulate as money.

If our currency were entirely of gold, and greater in value than $250,000,000, the excess would necessarily cease to circulate; it would either be hoarded for use at some future time, exported, or melted up into articles of jewelry. The fact that it may be put to other uses than that of money, thus prevents its value from depreciating.

In a country possessed of no great moneyed institutions, where little credit is given, and no debts incurred to be paid at distant periods, the evils of a depreciating currency are not so seriously felt as in a country differently circumstanced. If a dollar bill, starting at par in gold, is in the course of a year gradually diminished to fifty cents, it may perhaps have passed through hundreds of hands in the mean time, so that the loss of fifty cents has been divided among hundreds of people. But if, at the beginning of the year, an individual who did not foresee the depreciation, agreed to receive the bill as a gold dollar at the end of the year, he would thereby lose one-half.

As the currency depreciates prices must rise in

proportion, and, if the proper equilibrium to which prices tend is preserved, they will all rise in the same proportion. Thus, if one coat is worth as much as two pair of boots before the depreciation, it will still be worth two pair of boots afterward, unless some circumstance other than the depreciation affect the price.

Another relationship of value necessarily holds between the prices in gold and in currency of all commodities. If a coat is worth $20 in gold, $1 in gold worth $2 in currency, and three barrels of flour worth a coat, then one barrel of flour is worth 13\frac{1}{3}$ in currency. If the barrel of flour is worth but $10 in currency here, and $8 in gold in England, it will necessarily be exported until its price here rises, or the price in England falls so that the difference only pays for the risk and expense of shipping. Simple as these principles are, they are very imperfectly understood, else we should hear far less of talk about fictitious premium on gold, effects of speculation, &c.

As moneyed institutions rise, as large amounts of property take the form of debts, as banks, savings banks, insurance and trust companies, railroad corporations, and other institutions absorbing large sums of money for payment at distant periods begin to be established, then it is that a depreciated currency becomes really destructive. Let us see what was involved in that sweeping enactment which made bills a legal tender in payment of all private debts.

Three years ago 200 mechanics each put $100 in gold into a savings bank. The savings bank afterward loaned this $20,000 to a shipbuilder, who employed it in building a ship. He sends the ship to England and sells her for $22,000 in gold, making ten per cent. legitimate profit. By every principle of justice, $20,000 of the money belongs to the savings bank. But now the legal tender clause comes in and declares the builder relieved from the debt on payment of 20,000 paper dollars. He therefore buys these paper dollars with perhaps $8,000 in gold, pays them to the bank, and keeps the additional $12,000 for his own private use. He can cover Mrs. Shipper with diamonds, indulge in riotous living during the rest of the war, and furnish to the country a striking example of commercial prosperity.

A professional man, dependent entirely on his income for support, insured his life in order that his family might not be left penniless at his death. The life insurance company loans the money to Mr. Shoddy, who invests it in manufacturing capital. With the rise in gold Mr. Shoddy finds both his capital and profits apparently to increase in a corresponding ratio. When his debt is due he finds that he can sell one-half his stock for greenbacks sufficient to pay it, he retaining the other half, though it also rightfully belongs to the insurance company.

Banking capital suffers in the same way, unless the bank holds specie to the full amount of its capital. If a bank holds no specie, its capital and profits are in the form of an excess of debts due to the bank over those due from it, and whatever deteriorates the value of those debts deteriorates the capital in the same proportion. If it holds specie to the full amount of its capital and profits, then the debts due and those payable balance each other, and it suffers nothing from depreciation of the currency. It suffers in proportion to the excess of capital and profits over specie reserve.

Suppose, now, that a bank holding specie to the amount of one-tenth of its capital had, toward the end of 1861, refused to discount any more notes, called in all its paper, and thus collecting its entire capital in the form of specie, had locked that specie up, only drawing from it what was necessary to pay its regular semi-annual dividends in currency. For each share of $100, the cost of those dividends, supposing each to be three per cent. would have been as follows:

Jan., 1862	$3.00	July, 1863	$2.14
July, 1862	$2.70	Jan., 1864	$1.96
Jan., 1863	$2.14	July, 1864	$1.36

Total cost in gold $13.30, leaving $86.70 of the capital unimpaired, which would be worth, with gold at 2.20, $190 per share. As things actually stand, the stock of such a bank is only worth $112. Thus, by using their capital for the benefit of the public, the banks have, in three years, lost 40 per cent. on its entire amount, beside interest. Including interest, they have lost 50 per cent. This lost capital has not gone to the Government, but to that portion of the community who have done business on borrowed capital, and has of course caused their business to prosper in proportion.

Some astute economists hold that banks which hold a large percentage of specie have an interest in the rise of coin, because the coin in their vaults, and their stock also, will thereby increase in price. If the community coincide in opinion with those wiseacres; if owners of bank stock are satisfied with seeing their stock worth a great many dollars, without caring whether those dollars are themselves worth any thing or not; then the economists in question little dream how rich a mine of national wealth they have struck. Our country can be made the most powerful in the globe, our men transformed into giants, and our manufactures made to exceed those of all other nations put together, by very simple acts of Congress. In the first place let it be enacted that the gold dollar shall be reduced to one-fifth of its present weight, and all other coins in proportion; and that previous to the new coinage the present gold dollar shall be lawful money and legal tender for $5; the eagle for $50, and so on. The consequence will be that the price of all the real and personal property of the country will be increased five-fold. The man who was before worth only $2,000 will suddenly find himself worth $10,000; the real and personal estate of the country, instead of being worth only $16,000,000,000 will now be worth $80,000,000,000. It would be nothing more than fair to divide this enormous increase of $64,000,000,000 equally between the Government and the individual property holders; the former thus getting $32,000,000,000, and leaving the country more than twice as wealthy as in the beginning. This enormous sum would pay off our national debt, and enable us to become the first military power of the globe.

The act need not be confined to money value. It might also be enacted that hereafter the lawful foot should consist of only six inches instead of twelve; and that the pound should contain but two ounces instead of sixteen. Our people would then find themselves grown to the gigantic height of eleven or twelve feet, and our artillery would throw shot weighing thousands of pounds! What earthly power could take the field against men twelve feet high, using cannon throwing thousand-pound shot, backed by a Government with $32,000,000,000 of money? If the economists aforesaid are true to their principles they will answer NONE.

If all this were actually done, it is probable that a large part of the community would not be long in concluding that the apparent increase in the wealth of the country, the size of the man, and the weight of the artillery, was all fictitious; that a piece of gold had increased in price, not because it was worth any more than before, but because the dollar was worth less, just as the apparent increase in the height of the men proceeds from a shortening of the foot measure. It can hardly be necessary to tell any thinking man that this opinion is correct; that the real value of gold has not increased a jot since the beginning of the war, but rather diminished, because there is now less use for it; that it is now exported just as freely as ever, if not more so; and that bank stock which since 1860 has risen from par to 200 is really less valuable now than then.

Heretofore one distinguishing feature of civilized Governments has been the protection which they have afforded to property. They protect the owner not only in that which he holds in his own hands, but in that which he entrusts to others. The advantage which society thus gains is strikingly shown by an illustration of the "transmutatians of wealth" in Bowen's Political Economy. A laborer saves $100 from his earnings. "What will he do with this $100?" In a rude state of society among a half-civilized people, or under the government of a Turkish Pacha, property being insecure, he would probably obtain it in the form of gold or silver coin, and bury it in the corner of his cellar or garden. There, sure enough, it would remain without change, and therefore without income or increase. But in this country, in England, or in France, he would probably put it into the savings bank. He would thus benefit not only himself, by receiving interest on his money, but also the community, by placing $100 more capital at the disposal of the customers of the bank. The latter would be enabled to make more shares, bake more bread, and import more cloths.

Our own country will now have to be excepted from the list of those in which it is always desirable to invest coin in savings banks, rather than bury it under ground. The depositors in the savings banks of Massachusetts alone have been defrauded out of twenty million dollars of their savings, which they would have kept had they buried them. It is impossible to form an accurate estimate of the entire losses sustained by the creditor class of the community, but the following is an exhibit of some items. Debts due the following institutions have been diminished by 50 per cent. of the amount given:

Banks of Issue, ...	$280,000,000
Savings Banks, . . .	100,000,000
Insurance and Trust Companies, .	50,000,000

If to these we add the losses sustained by individuals, we shall probably have a sum total of $1,000,000,000, one-half of which has changed hands by the legal tender act. What a commentary is this on our financial policy—that the owners of property to the extent of $1,000,000,000 would have done better to bury their property in the earth than suffer it to be loaned the public for the public benefit! What would we have thought in 1861 at such a conversation as the following between an owner of bank stock and an individual of sufficient prescience to see what was coming?

"I advise you, sir, speedily to sell your bank stock for coin, and keep that coin for three years or more; for if you keep your stock, it and all its proceeds will then be worth little more than half as much as the gold."

"What catastrophe is coming? Our stock is nearly all in the form of well-secured promissory notes of sound commercial men, and I cannot conceive how they should fail to pay us."

"No catastrophe at all is coming. Your property will be legislated out of your hands so smoothly and gently that most of your stockholders will never know it. They will, at the same time, be furnished with a pair of magnifying spectacles which will make every dollar look like a quarter-eagle; so that when their stock is reduced to one-half, it will look more valuable than ever."

"It will then, I suppose, be seized by the Government."

"There you are mistaken. The Government will suffer with you.'

"Then what *will* become of our property?"

This question is worth considering. What has become of all this $500,000,000 which the moneyed institutions and individual creditors have lost? It has not been destroyed. It has passed into the possession of those men who, during the time that gold was rising, were doing business on borrowed capital. For every debtor there must be a creditor; there must be as much money owing as being owed. How the wealth has changed hands may be seen from the examples of the shipbuilder and the manufacturer already cited. Another illustration may be given in the case of an importer. In May, 1864, an importer borrows $20,000 from a bank, and buys foreign exchange with the money to pay for cloths in England. In sixty days his cloths arrive in New York. The premium on gold, in the mean time, has risen from 80 per cent. to 150 per cent. The price of his goods has increased in a corresponding ratio; they are worth 40 per cent. more in currency than they would have been two months previously. He sells out, and finds that, in addition to the regular profits of trade which he would have enjoyed had there been no advance in gold, he has made 40 per cent. on his entire outlay solely by the rise in gold, or, to speak more accurately, the fall in U. S. notes.

In what respect, let me ask, is this importer better than the "heartless speculator" of Wall Street, who "seeks to coin money out of the national misfortunes"? He has made his money, practically, in the same way, namely, by buying gold, and sixty days afterward selling, not indeed the gold, but the cloth bought with the gold, which amounts to the same thing. Thus every importer of foreign goods is, per force, a "speculator for the rise," whether he will or no. Is it wonderful that thousands, who would otherwise devote themselves to honest industry, are seduced into the giddy rounds of speculation when they see fortunes made so rapidly? And who is most to blame, the man seduced, or the system which seduces him by continuing a policy which offers such temptations?

As favorable a view as we can take of the legal tender act is that it enacts, in substance, as follows: *That whenever any debt is discharged within the United States the creditor shall forfeit to the debtor such percentage of the debt as is equal to the depreciation of legal tender notes since the debt was contracted.* This, in fact, is the simple sum and substance of the enactment. It made every promissory note, every bank bill, every dollar of bank stock, every bond of every state and railroad corporation, and, indeed, every promise to pay money, a *real unavoidable* bet, which the creditor wins when gold goes down, and the debtor when gold goes up. This, in fact, is the result of every system of irredeemable legal tender paper, and must continue to be while human nature remains as it is.

It must be remembered that, in the general confiscation of fifty per cent. of all old debts which happen to be payable now, the Government gets no share whatever of the spoils. The shipbuilder has pocketed the savings of the mechanics, the manufacturer those of the life insurance company, and the importer the capital of the bank, but the Government nothing at all. Had we enacted that all debts due in the country should be paid through the Government, the creditor paying the Government coin, and Government paying the debtor in legal tender notes, so as to gain the amount of the depreciation, the creditor would have had the satisfaction of knowing his loss to be the public gain. As things are, he has no satisfaction whatever.

To a lover of justice the discussion of such a system of spoliation, from a purely utilitarian point of view, must be repulsive in the extreme. No man who believes that honesty is the best policy; no man who believes in a moral government of the universe; no man who believes that the laws of nature always act to preserve the good and destroy the evil, will ask for any other judgment on the system than that which will be pronounced by his own conscience. But it will be instructive to trace all this injustice to its economic effects, present and future, if only to show how we are to be punished for transgressing the moral law.

It is plain that, while gold has been rising from par to a premium of one hundred and thirty per cent., the creditor class of the community, represented by the owners of bank stock, depositors in savings banks, holders of bonds and mortgages, and the frugal poor who have loaned their savings, have, on the whole, been subjected to heavy and unjust losses, while the debtor class, represented by those who live beyond their income, or do business on borrowed capital, have made heavy and illegitimate profits. Owing to the different functions of these two classes in the social economy, these gains and losses are productive of effects which vitally concern the best interests of society, and are, therefore, well worthy the serious consideration both of the philosopher and the statesman.

The debtor class, having been from time to time relieved of a percentage of their equitable liability, have found less difficulty than usual in meeting their obligations. Hence there have been fewer failures than common, as well as larger profits, and unusual business prosperity. For the country is naturally considered prosperous when there are few failures and large profits. The corresponding losses of the creditor are productive of little inconvenience to him, and are almost entirely overlooked. Productive of little inconvenience because the very fact of the creditor's willingness and ability to resign the use of his property to his neighbor shows that he can do without it. No one loans money for a month, a year, or a term of years, unless he is able to forego the use of all except the interest during that length of time; consequently, if the principal of his loan is impaired, or even wholly destroyed, it does not interfere with the regular course of his business. His loss is overlooked because it takes the form of a depreciation of the currency in which his debt is payable; nominally he loses nothing, because his debt is worth as many dollars as ever. Thus the losses which counterbalance the profits of the debtor are entirely lost sight of by those who take a merely superficial view.

The debtor, being more inclined to enjoy his money than to lay it up, very naturally spends a large portion of his profits in gratifying his desires. Hence an unusual consumption of luxuries, and another sign of prosperity. It is as if a provident farmer, who had been laying up a supply of choice fruit for sale, should be compelled to divide that fruit among such of his neighbors as did not believe that the products of the orchard were intended for any other use than immediate enjoyment. The tables of the community might be greatly improved for a week. But at the end of the week the wealth would have been consumed. A nation can no more "eat its cake and have it too" than can an individual. Thus the depreciating currency encourages the consumption and enjoyment of wealth rather than its preservation. This is the real nature and effect of the prosperity which is so attractive when we do not look below the surface.

When Government wishes a loan, it must apply to the creditor class. Without a temper and disposition peculiar to this class no government could ever borrow. There must be a willingness on the part of owners of property to forego the present enjoyment of wealth, and part with it for a long series of years, in consideration of receiving a small fraction of it annually in the form of interest. The more universal this disposition to lend, the better the terms on which the Government can borrow. The Government ought, therefore, to encourage this disposition by making all property in the form of debts as secure as possible. The transfers of the ownership of this great reserve power to the business and debtor class, not only takes it from those who are disposed to *lend* and gives it to those who are disposed to *use* and spend on their own account, but discourages that disposition without which Government can never borrow.

The delusive prosperity caused by this transfer is only *the fattening of the canker-worm which is eating out the very vitals of public credit.*

The writer has no disposition to hide the good or exaggerate the evil of the measures under consideration. He has shown that the legal tender notes, or rather their depreciation, has promoted commercial prosperity and the general enjoyment of wealth by the community. It was only right to show, in addition, that this additional enjoyment arose from the consumption of wealth which would otherwise have been saved or turned into the channels of war.

So, on the other hand, he is prepared to admit that, had our business during the war been conducted on a specie basis, the commercial and business depression, and a general inability on the part of the debtor class to command the usual amount of the necessaries and luxuries of life, would have been inevitable. Still more marked would have been this seeming poverty, had the war been carried on mainly by taxation, as it is claimed it should. But it is contended that this depression would not have indicated any diminution of the real power or wealth of the country, and that all its evils would have been temporary. To illustrate this, let us consider that class of debtors whose case would excite most sympathy—farmers who had mortgaged their farms. Real estate, bearing about the same nominal price now as before the war, and therefore worth only half as much in gold, would have fallen considerably had there been no depreciation of the currency. But it would not have fallen to one-half, because part of the actual fall is, no doubt, due to the unusual profits of trade and speculation having stimulated the diversion of capital into those channels, rather than into the more solid investment of real estate and government bonds.

But although the farmer might thus be subject to a heavy and unforeseen loss, if obliged to sell his farm in order to pay the mortgages, yet his ability to make money from it would be but slightly diminished, nay, would not be diminished at all except by the war taxes. Unless he mortgaged on speculation, intending to sell in order to redeem the mortgage, he must have calculated that he could redeem it from the produce of the farm. The available produce being diminished by the war tax, he would have been obliged to deny himself and his family the enjoyment of the usual luxuries, and perhaps even some of the necessaries of life, and, at the same time, to work harder, so as to produce more corn, hay, and beef. Thus he would have suffered; thus the class he represents, namely, men doing business on borrowed capital, would have suffered had the currency remained as valuable as specie.

But the important point is that this suffering would have involved an increase in the ability of the nation to carry on the war, just as the enjoyment permitted by the depreciation has caused a diminution of that ability. In fact, the farmer, obliged to raise more wheat, hay, and beef, will have more to offer the Government, and, obliged to deny himself in clothing, will be less a competitor with the Government in the purchase of that article; Government will, therefore, be able to purchase it more cheaply.

Still, saying nothing of injustice, it may be thought that, if the creditor class are not sensible of their loss, much harm will not be done after all. The unenlightened man, who knows nothing of political economy, does not know that he is defrauded of his just rights by being paid his old debts in paper. How, then, can he be discouraged from making future loans?

Such a view, though specious, would be entirely fallacious. Whatever theory may be adopted respecting the moral government of the universe, the experience of mankind in all ages shows that any evasion of the great law of compensation is an impossibility. In the case in question, ignorance of political economy can no more prevent the legitimate effect of a wrong economical measure than ignorance of toxicology can prevent the action of a poison. We have poisoned the springs of our true wealth and greatness, and we shall most assuredly suffer the legitimate consequences, though every man in the country believes and proclaims that the poison was a healthy and necessary stimulant. Take, for example, the case of the man who is unconscious of being wronged. Suppose there is a community of such people. If they are not sensible of their loss, its effect will be all the more lasting. The laborer who put his earnings into the savings bank now sees that his neighbor, who turned his into gold which he kept in a stocking, has somehow done better than himself. Not understanding the causes which have brought about this state of things, he will not know when they cease to exist. He will, therefore, during the rest of his life substitute the stocking for the savings bank, and perhaps teach his children to do the same.

Though specie payments should be resumed, our entire financial system restored to a healthy state, and the savings bank patronized by all, with every war and rumor of war, with every whisper of a suspension or a financial crisis, there will be a general panic among the poor and ignorant, and a general run on the banks to realize all notes and securities in the form of specie. And if public opinion permits a suspension of specie payments, speculation in gold will be resumed in all its vigor, in remembrance of the enormous profits made by this operation in times past. So long as men remember, without disgust, the iniquitous decisions of those judges who have disgraced the very name of LAW, and legalized acts of perfidy which would put a savage to the blush, by declaring our paper money a legal tender in discharge of the most solemn contracts to deliver a specified weight of gold or silver coin, so long will entire confidence between man and man be impossible. The evil will be corrected only when the public at large view the acts and the system now under consideration with such reprobation that *every one shall feel a repetition of them to be impossible.* For how can any man receive with confidence a promise from his neighbor to pay a specified sum in gold coin at the end of a term of years, when he does not know but that an ignorant legislature and prejudiced judiciary may, in the mean time, entirely relieve that neighbor from all obligation to fulfil the contract?

In his first annual report on the finances, not a month before the suspension of specie payments, Mr. Chase warned Congress of the possible consequences of a system of government circulating notes in the following prophetic words.

"The temptation, especially great in times of pressure and danger, to issue notes without adequate provision for redemption; the ever-present liability to be called on for redemption beyond means however carefully provided and managed; the hazard of panics precipitating demands for coin concentrated on a few points and a single fund; the risk of a depreciated, depreciating, and finally worthless paper money; the immeasurable evils of dishonored public faith and national bankruptcy; all these are possible consequences of the adoption of a system of government circulation."

Suppose, now, that our paper money system had been expressly designed to produce all the evils so graphically described by the Honorable Secretary, in what respect would it have been different from what it actually was? See how exactly it seemed calculated to promote the four principal evils:

"The temptation, especially great in times of pressure and danger, to issue notes without *adequate* provision for redemption."

This temptation was yielded to by issuing several hundred millions of notes without any provision at all for redemption.

"The hazard of panics, precipitating demands for coin concentrated on a few points and a single fund."

This hazard was indeed most effectually guarded against. But how? By letting the noteholders know in advance that any demands for coin, deliberate or precipitous, would be a waste of time and words. So the times when there would have been such panics were indicated only by the upward jumps in the price of gold. This was avoiding the hazard in the same way that a man who should jump overboard in mid ocean from a leaky ship would avoid the hazard of being carried down with her.

"The risk of a depreciated, depreciating, and finally worthless paper money."

The great risk and great evil of a depreciating paper money are found in the losses it entails on those moneyed institutions in which the savings of the nation are invested. Accordingly, the currency, having been left to depreciate as fast as it would, three-fourths of the banking capital of the country, all the State debts, and nearly the entire assets of all savings banks and life insurance companies, were fastened to it by the legal tender clause. These interests have followed the currency half way to ruin, and, should it finally become worthless, must be ruined with it.

"The immeasurable evils of dishonored public faith and national bankruptcy."

The Treasury deliberately refused to pay notes issued by authority of law and declared payable on demand by the same authority. A law was then passed, under the operation of which paper money was a legal tender, not only in payment of these notes, but in return for one hundred millions of gold coin paid into the Treasury by the people. If by "dishonored public faith" the Honorable Secretary did not mean a failure to pay the notes, what did he mean? And what did he mean by "national bankruptcy"? Is this calamity possible while it is possible to print the words "United States will pay the bearer —— dollars"?

It is one of the embarrassments of our situation that we cannot restore our finances to a healthy condition without producing effects injurious to the business interests of the country. Opposite causes must produce opposite effects. If, in consequence of a sudden improvement in government credit, our currency should become as valuable as gold, we should experience a commercial revulsion proportioned to the excitement consequent upon the depreciation of the currency. Those trading on borrowed capital would be subject to heavy losses, and traders of every class would be obliged to sell their goods below the nominal cost. The derangement of trade thus produced will obstruct the operations of supply and demand throughout their whole course, as the stopping of a single company in a marching column of troops will throw the whole into confusion.

But the real interests of the nation would not, in the end, suffer by this revulsion. If its effects are the reverse of those formerly described in their superficial aspect, they will be equally so when we consider their ulterior effects upon the stability of the Government, and the highest economic interests of the country. The Government will gain by being enabled to buy and borrow on better terms than before. The real prosperity of the country will not be diminished, but rather increased, because we will then turn our attention to saving rather than enjoying our wealth. Indeed, if every dollar of our paper circulation were annihilated to-morrow, it would be a very serious question whether it were not the best thing for the nation that could happen ; whether we would not come out of the commercial crash which would be the result a wiser people, in a better position to fulfil our mission to the human race.

7

CHAPTER VI.

NECESSITY OF PAPER MONEY—THE LESSONS OF HISTORY.

In the last two chapters we have set forth the evils which have flowed and must continue to flow from our issues of irredeemable paper money. Respecting the character and extent of these evils there will be little difference of opinion. All must concede their gravity to be such that the measure can be justified only on the ground of imperious necessity.

But this is only one side of the case. The measure was adopted under the pressure of a great emergency; and in an emergency the very best course may be productive of many evils, and subject to a quarto volume of objections. Hence it will be premature to pass judgment on it until we have inquired whether it has been productive of any good to compensate for all these evils. Have these notes enabled us to put more men into the field, or to build more ships? Have they performed any important office of war, which could not have been performed without them? Public opinion seems inclined to answer these questions in the affirmative. What is the foundation of this opinion? If it is correct we can certainly show how the good has been effected. But a satisfactory exposition of the mode of operation of the legal tender notes, showing in what way they have performed the functions of money better than coin, or notes convertible into coin, is a desideratum with which the friends of the measure have never supplied us.

In the absence of such an exposition the question must be considered on its own merits. The two great authorities to which we appeal are reason and experience. The friends of the measure are fond of appealing in a vague and general way to experience, by saying that no great war was ever carried on without paper money. A refutation of this assertion would involve us in a useless verbal dispute unless we could first agree what wars should be considered "great wars," and what sort of evidences of indebtedness should be considered "paper money." Paper money has indeed been used as a medium of exchange in some great wars, and it is very pertinent to our present purpose to inquire whether it has aided the belligerents in their efforts. The three systems of paper money best known to us are:—

The "Continental money" of our revolution.

The assignats of the first French revolution.

The bank money of England during the Napoleonic wars.

The last is so essentially different from the other issues, our own included, that no instructive comparison can be made with it. No paper money was issued by the British Government to pay off its debts except very limited amounts of interest-bearing "exchequer bills." The circulating notes were issued by the Bank of England, which was alone responsible for their redemption. As this institution always held in specie, and the notes of solvent individuals, the means of making good all its obligations whenever the law restricting specie payments should be repealed or cease to operate, any serious depreciation of the notes was impossible except as a result of bad management on the part of the bank, or a panic on the part of the people. It was simply an instance of a bank suspension of specie payments, and we have seen how different this is from a government suspension. Its effect was not, like the latter, to encourage the exportation of specie in exchange for luxuries, but to keep it locked up ready for any emergency.

The paper money experience of our revolutionary ancestors and the French Republic will be reviewed, not for the purpose of giving a detailed history of the origin, progress, and final fall of the money, but to learn to what extent, and in what way, it assisted them in the efforts they were obliged to make to maintain their governments, and to see whether our circumstances are so like theirs, that our paper money extends a similar help to us.

NECESSITY OF PAPER MONEY.

The Continental Congress first authorized the issue of certain "bills of credit" in 1775. These bills were paper money, pure and simple. They bore no interest, were not convertible into any kind of bonds, were not secured by any thing but the promise of the power which issued them, and after the first six millions were issued no time was fixed for their redemption. They were simple certificates that the bearer thereof was entitled to a certain number of "Spanish milled dollars." After the issue exceeded a certain limit, the inevitable process of depreciation commenced. It continued slowly, but regularly, throughout the whole revolutionary war. Every fall in the value of the paper gave rise to larger and larger issues, until, finally, $200,000,000 of it were in circulation, and all hope of its redemption vanished. In 1781-'2 it gradually disappeared from circulation altogether, and coin flowed in to take its place. No provision was ever made for its redemption.

These are the essential facts of the case. Our revolutionary war was carried on and brought to a successful issue by means of this depreciated, depreciating, and finally worthless paper money. But let us see how. Were there neither taxes nor loans?

With the issue of every bill a loan was effected, and a debt contracted. When Congress bought from an individual a musket, or a barrel of pork, giving him a bill in exchange, it borrowed from him on the spot, and the bill was the certificate of indebtedness. Suppose the bill was worth $20 in coin when issued, and that when the holder passed it off again it was worth but $19, then he virtually paid a tax of $1 toward the discharge of the debt, and received $19 worth of some article for the remainder. If the bill was worth but $18 when it changed hands again, the second holder paid another dollar tax, as he received but $18 worth of goods for it, while he had given $19. Thus, the bill itself collected a tax equivalent to its depreciation from every man through whose hands it passed. And since every bill issued must have been held by some one during the whole time it was depreciating to nothing, the sum total of the taxes thus collected must have been the equivalent of the sum total of the supplies it originally purchased for the Government. Thus the tax was, virtually, a very irregular one on *sales*, equivalent, on the average, to the percentage of depreciation every time the bill changed hands.

It is now, I hope, perfectly plain that so far as the people at large were concerned, they could just as well have afforded to furnish all the supplies bought with the money as a direct tax; nay, could have afforded them much better in this form, because the tax could have been graduated so as to fall more equally. As was remarked in a previous chapter, the tax was apportioned according to men's confidence in the good faith of the country, because, the greater this confidence, the more they would be disposed to hold on to the money in hope of its final redemption.

But whether that assemblage of men who constituted the Continental Congress could have put in operation a system of taxation which would have collected the supplies bought with the paper money is an entirely different question. Their office was advisory, not mandatory. Any laws they might have enacted would have had to depend on the separate State authorities for their execution. This circumstance alone would have rendered it extremely difficult to put any general scheme of taxation into operation. Again, the use of paper money was a most easy and certain means of collecting the tax. Neither assessors nor collectors were necessary. There were no applications for abatement, no legal technicalities to hinder the execution of the law. Once issue the note, and *somebody* would most assuredly pay. If not the right man, then the wrong one. Finally, much as the admission may reflect on the good sense of our ancestors, it must be conceded that men submitted to a tax in this form, who would not willingly have submitted to one so heavy in any other form.

All these conclusions harmonize completely with those to which we were led in the chapter on "the financial elements of military strength." It was there shown, in general, that the military power which a people are able to put forth is not increased by the money circulating through the channels of business. This general principle is illustrated by the fact that our ancestors really paid as heavy taxes to carry on the revolutionary war as if no paper money had been used. If they had not been able to sustain the taxes they would not have been able to furnish the supplies in exchange for the money.

But it is not intended to maintain that no Government, no man or collection of men endowed temporarily or permanently with authority, can ever add to their power by an issue of paper money. In proportion as the *Government* and the *people* constitute two separate and distinct interests, in that same proportion may circumstances arise to make an issue of paper money by the former advisable. Thus a king, who finds his expenses to exceed his income, and whose subjects are more noted for lack of judgment than for loyalty; or a collection of men, like our Continental Congress, charged with the interests of a people, but unable to put the machinery of taxation into operation, may promote their objects by issuing bills of credit, though the real interests of the country will most assuredly suffer. It is very clear that the relation of the Government of the United States to the people thereof is not of either of these characters. Our Government is a firmly-established one, with practically unlimited power to levy taxes. Its interests are identical with those of the people. It is to be sincerely hoped that our people have too much good sense to desire to be cheated out of a tax which they would not pay directly.

Thus, a comparison of our circumstances with those of our ancestors does not indicate that our legal tender notes were either necessary or expedient. Still more conclusive is the experience of the French Republic.

The "assignats" and "mandats" of the French revolution bore a greater resemblance to our legal tender notes than any other well-known system of paper money. Substitute government bonds for landed estates, and the resemblance is complete. The circumstances which seemed to make their issue necessary, were of the same general nature with those which gave rise to our notes, only the difficulties of the situation were far more grave and far more real. Indeed, the deplorable state of the French finances during the reign of Louis XVI. was one great cause of the revolution. The taxes were all paid by the "third estate," the nobles and clergy being exempt. They were so heavy in proportion to the productive powers of the people, that industry was nearly paralyzed. At the same time the expenses of the Government were greatly in excess of its revenue. The deficit was made up by "farming out" future taxes to capitalists who supplied the Government with money at exorbitant rates of interest. The debt thus increased from year to year, without any corresponding increase in the productive power of the people. Specie had almost ceased to circulate. The king had to coin his plate into money. The wisdom and economy of Neckar were insufficient to the task of making both ends meet. Such was the state of affairs when the States-General commenced the work of remodelling the Government and social system of France.

The first vigorous attempt to provide a remedy for these evils, was made in 1790. A wholesale confiscation of the entire landed property of the Church was decreed. The objects of the Assembly are thus set forth by Thiers:

"To deprive a too powerful body of a large portion of their estates, divide these estates in the best possible way, so as to allow a large part of the poorer classes to become landed proprietors; finally, by the same operation to extinguish the public debt, and reëstablish order in the finances: such was the object of the Assembly, and they felt its importance too strongly to cower before obstacles."

But, how could the possession of landed property be made to contribute to the military power of the nation? This was the insoluble problem which the Assembly attacked. It was perfectly clear that to throw such quantities of land on the market at once would greatly depress its price, not only from lack of disposition on the part of the people to buy so much, but from lack of ability to pay for it. So the attempt was made to obtain the value of the lands indirectly, by issuing *assignats*, evidences of indebtedness, bearing a certain daily interest, and entitling the holder to confiscated lands equal in value to the face of the note, just as our notes entitle the holders to certain United States bonds, To give them a still greater value, they were declared a legal tender. Neckar, warning the Assembly of the consequences of the measure, was thrown overboard, and finally compelled to flee the country, much as a young profligate might dismiss his physician for pointing out the inevitable consequences of his acts.

At first, the new scheme worked well, as such schemes always do. The people were delighted to be relieved from the visits of the tax gatherer. The assignats paid off the public creditors, purchased army supplies, and kept the Government going. They furnished the people with *money*, the great national want. Very soon, however, the nation had all the money it wanted, and thereafter the assignats must depend for their value, not on being a legal tender, but on being convertible into land, of which they were the representitive. The falsity of the theory on which they were issued, now became manifest. The Assembly did not want to glut the market with land, so they glut it with the representative of land instead. How the representative could have a greater value than the thing represented; why any man would give a larger consideration for a certificate entitling him to land than he would for the land itself, they did not ask.

The baneful effects which followed, the continual rise in price of all the necessaries of life; the almost total stoppage of productive industry, and the substitution of attempts to make money by any other means than honest industry, the only real source of wealth; the vain attempts of the Convention, backed by the mob and the guillotine, to fix a maximum of prices; the rage and misery of the half-starved populace; all these illustrate the folly of human nature, but do not prove that the assignats really did no good whatever for the Republic.

The circumstances of their fall are conclusive on this point. A defect in their form, which in fact was pointed out by Neckar when they was first proposed, became evident during their depreciation. The land in which they were redeemable rose in price with every thing else (though, of course, not in the same ratio), so that in 1796 an assignat would buy a small fraction of the land it would have bought originally. To remedy this objection the assignats were withdrawn, and the "*mandats*" were issued in lieu of them, at the rate of one franc in mandats for twenty in assignats. The new bills entitled the holder to receive the lands at their valuation in 1790. They therefore bore the same relation to the assignats that our original legal tender notes, expressly convertible, dollar for dollar, into five-twenty bonds, bear to the present notes, which are merely receivable in payment of loans, on any terms the Government may prescribe. But the people had become so disgusted with the paper money that the mandats did not circulate as many months as the assignats had years. Refused by all as money, they were bought up by speculators for investment in lands. After a vain contest, the Directory were obliged to give way and return to a specie basis. The mandats were received and paid out by the Government only at their market rates for coin, which soon became the only currency of the nation.

This happened in 1796, in the midst of the first Italian campaign, when the twenty years' struggle of France with the other European powers was but fairly begun. If our modern theories, or rather our modern rejuvenation of old theories, of the necessity of paper money are correct, this downfall of the circulating medium must have been disastrous in the extreme. But, so far is this from being the case, that productive industry rapidly recovered from the depression of the paper money. Men raised corn and made bread in full confidence that no mob would punish them for their pains, by compelling them to part with it for worthless rags. The war was continued nineteen years without any attempt to issue more paper money, and from 1796 till now nothing but coin has been a legal tender in France.

Looking back, then, at the actual effects of paper money in past generations, and at the actual services rendered by it; weighing justly all its benefits and all its evils, it must be conceded that it warns us to avoid it much more forcibly than it invites us to adopt it, and that it has never lent to any Government a help of which we were in need when we tried it. It has simply proved the intoxicating cup of nations. As a bottle of wine seemingly invigorates the laborer, and diffuses new life through every vein, so does an issue of irredeemable paper money stimulate commerce, and give a new impulse to business of almost every kind. The first effects are so good that a universal cry for more soon rises from the entire body politic. Government is certain to yield to the temptation. More is issued, and yet more. The point at which the stimulus becomes clearly unhealthy is as well marked in the case of the nation as in that of the individual. There is a universal disposition to *buy*, a universal demand for money to buy with, but a growing indisposition to *make* or *produce* by honest industry.

When this state of things reaches its inevitable termination, the depression is as great as was the previous excitement. As the bones, muscles, and nerves of the individual are still entire after a fit of drunkenness, so are the nation's elements of material wealth. But the elements of moral power, which alone can make wealth contribute to our real happiness, are destroyed. Mutual confidence, public faith, private honor, frugal industry, all are gone like the nervous energies of the drunkard.

CHAPTER VII.

WERE THE LEGAL TENDER NOTES NECESSARY?

HAVING seen to what extent the issue of our circulating notes is sustained by the precedents of history, it is now proposed to consider them on their own merits, and examine the official arguments with which they have been sustained. The measure presents four features which, for the sake of clearness, will be considered separately. The questions to which these features give rise are as follows:

1. Was it expedient to issue notes at all?
2. Was it necessary that they should not be redeemable in coin?
3. That they should be a legal tender for the principal of the public debt?
4. That they should be a legal tender in payment of private debts?

That the issue of notes sufficient in amount to form the entire circulating medium of the country was *expedient*, cannot, I think, be successfully controverted.* Such an issue is equivalent to a loan

---

* It will be understood that the discussion of constitutional objec-

from the people of its entire amount, without interest. Before the war this advantage had been monopolized by the banks, and Mr. Chase, in his first annual report (December, 1861) well remarks that "it deserves consideration whether sound policy does not require that the advantages of this loan be transferred, in part, at least, from the banks, representing only the interests of the stockholders, to the Government representing the aggregate interests of the whole people." It is hard to see why, when the Government was in so great a strait, the entire advantages of the loan should not have been transferred to it. Let us look at the exact nature of this loan, as much misapprehension exists respecting it.

Its maximum amount may vary from $200,000,000 to $300,000,000. The real advantages which it is possible to obtain from the issue of circulating notes are exhausted when their amount reaches this limit. Issue more, and they will come back for redemption if redeemable, or depreciate if they are not. We may, indeed, in the latter case, adopt the miserable plan of recklessly issuing more and more, thus collecting an indirect tax by their depreciation, as our revolutionary forefathers did. In that case, however, we must finally either repudiate the notes, or redeem them by collecting the

---

tions to an issue of notes by the Government is foreign to our present purpose. Taking the power to issue notes for granted, we are only inquiring how far it is expedient to exercise it.

tax all over again for the benefit of the last holders.

I repeat it: a loan of say $250,000,000, during the pleasure of the Government, without interest, is the sole advantage to be derived from the issue of notes. After this loan is contracted, *we are in the same position with respect to future loans as if no notes at all had been issued.* Unfortunately, however, the notes were expected also to facilitate new loans. Such a mistake could never have been made by any one who knew enough of political economy to have a clear comprehension of the functions of money. But for it we should never have experienced any of the evils of a redundant currency. That it was made and acted on is evident from the tenor of Mr. Chase's first two annual reports. In his report of December, 1862, he says, with reference to the possibility of negotiating loans of coin ten months before:

" Careful inquiries satisfied the Secretary that the first $60,000,000 could not be had, in coin, at better rates than a dollar in bonds for eighty cents in money; and that each succeeding loan would involve submission to increasingly disadvantageous terms. To obtain the first $60,000,000 would require, therefore, an issue of bonds to the amount of $75,000,000, and, of course, an increase of the public debt by the same sum; the next $60,000,000 would require perhaps $90,000,000 in bonds and debt; and the next $60,000,000, if obtainable at all, would require perhaps $120,000,000. It was easy to see that on this road utter discredit and paralysis would soon be reached. The adoption of a plan of finance involving such consequences was not compatible with the Secretary's ideas of public duty."

This specification of the terms on which the Government could borrow coin is not quoted for the purpose of refuting it, because its correctness does not affect the question under discussion. But it may be remarked, parenthetically, that events have shown the disadvantages which would have attended loans of coin to be greatly exaggerated. The "inquiries" seem to have been made at a moment of great general depression. Two months after they were made, and eight months before their result was communicated to Congress in the above paragraph, the six per cent. bonds brought very nearly par in coin, as will be seen from the table on pages 108, 109 (Chapter IV.). And in 1863, when, had the results of the inquiry been correct, the bonds would have been worth but fifty per cent. in coin, they were worth eighty. Moreover, subsequent experience has shown that the skilful negotiation of sixty millions of bonds at once need not depress their price more than five per cent.

A skilful negotiation is one conducted so as to avoid the accumulation of large quantities of coin. It is not denied that if, in effecting the three loans of coin of $60,000,000 each, the policy of the Treasury had been to keep all the coin locked up, instead of paying it out, the effects might have been as unfavorable as the honorable Secretary had predicted. But if the gold had been disbursed as fast as received, it would have been just as available for a new loan as it was before, so that the price of the bonds could have fallen only in consequence of a real depreciation of the government credit.

But whether the amount of bonds necessary to command $180,000,000 in coin would or would not have been as great as estimated, does not affect the question now under discussion. The only logical conclusion from the Secretary's statement was that it would never do to attempt the sale of bonds at all. Unfortunately, however, instead of accepting this conclusion, he goes on to consider whether it would be advisable to receive the notes of the State banks in lieu of coin, and gives very forcible reasons in the negative, which, however, derive their whole force from the circumstance that the banks had suspended specie payments. Finally, he concludes that in the legal tender notes we have a currency " with which, until the close of the war at least, loans and taxes may be paid to the Government, debts to individuals discharged, and the business of the country transacted." In all this it is implied that some kinds of currency may be employed more advantageously than others in the negotiation of bonds.

Now, no principle of Political Economy is more firmly established, both by reason and experience, than this; that money is not a creator of value, and can never permanently alter the relative value of commodities. To apply this principle to the present case, let us admit that while there is in existence in the country a certain amount of gold, $100 in bonds would have brought in the market only $50 in coin. To give the advocates of the currency as strong a case as possible, let us suppose that under the same circumstances the bond could be sold for $100 in currency. What would follow? Simply this, that $50 in gold would be worth in the market as much as $100 in paper; and that the former would therefore be at 100 per cent. premium. No one can maintain that $100 in paper and $50 in coin can be the market equivalent of the same thing, and yet not the equivalent of each other. And gold being at 100 per cent. premium, of course $100 in gold will buy as much flour, clothing, gunpowder, or iron, as $200 in paper. In one word, if the country is more willing to loan paper than gold, it can be only because it values the gold higher than the paper; and, this being the case, it will give more munitions of war for the gold than for the paper in exactly the same proportion.

It is very true that the Government could pay off old debts with a smaller issue of bonds by issuing depreciated paper, for the simple reason that the creditors could not help themselves. Thus, for a long time after gold rises, Government may by this system be in the actual receipt of goods at old prices. But, in contracting future debts, we may be sure that the contractor will charge for the depreciation, if he does not add on a good percentage in addition to compensate himself for the uncertainty. Finally, when gold falls, Government will have to pay high prices for about the same length of time it paid low prices during the rise, so that in the end the compensation will be complete.

If Government does not now give twice as much for every thing it wants as at the beginning of the war, the fact affords no argument against the position laid down. The large scale on which we are now manufacturing war material; the labor-saving devices which have been introduced; the introduction of female labor; the efforts of the country to supply its armies in the most economical way; all these circumstances operate to make the absolute cost of war material much less than in the beginning, when we were suddenly called upon for these immense supplies without any previous preparation. Consequently, had specie payments been continued, it is reasonably to be expected that we should now be manufacturing war material at a much cheaper rate than at first. What is maintained is, that *now* we are paying twice as high for every thing we buy as if we paid in gold. Even if we could not buy half as cheap for gold directly, we could indirectly by selling the gold for notes to buy with.

What the Government really gives in exchange for its supplies is its bonds, as a shoemaker really supplies himself with necessaries by making shoes.

The money which is paid into the Treasury for bonds, and then paid out again for supplies, serves no purpose except that of making and equalizing the exchanges, and enabling the Government to buy from the cheapest market, whether the seller wants bonds or not, and to sell bonds to the highest bidder, whether that bidder can furnish supplies or not. If the contractors who supply the Government were the same persons who wanted all the bonds, there would be no need at all of money.

Thus, the only necessary restrictions respecting the money with which loans should be negotiated, are those imposed by considerations of convenience, namely, (1) that the money should be easy to handle, (2) of equal value at all times, and (3) of equal value all over the country. The first condition is best fulfilled by paper, but coin would be subject to no serious inconvenience in this respect, because all large payments to or from the Government would have been made by checks, without actually handling the coin.

By some singular hallucination, it seemed to be taken for granted that after the suspension of specie payments it was no longer possible for the Government to borrow coin. This was considered the fundamental fact on which our policy would have to be based. Gold had "*disappeared!*" A stranger, ignorant of chemistry, would have derived the impression that, through some carelessness on the part of the public, our $300,000,000 in gold had all been suffered to evaporate. But the gold was still in the hands of the people and the banks. The very fact that it had disappeared from circulation, ought to make it more easy to borrow large sums, because the owners no longer needed it for money, and therefore could all the better afford to lend it. It is very true that during the temporary panic caused by the suspension, there would have been a general disposition to hold on to gold rather than pass it off at par. But why? Simply for fear on the part of the owners that Government would acquiesce in the suspension, for fear gold would be at a premium, for fear that if they parted with it they would not get it back again; in one word, for fear of the very things that actually were done! To conquer this difficulty it was only necessary for the Government to exhibit a bold and inflexible determination to continue its operations on a specie basis, irrespective of the doings of the banks, and thus dispel the fears in question. The holders of gold would soon have found it to be only so much idle capital lying on their hands, and would therefore have been desirous to exchange it for something which would yield a profit. Yet, so deeply has the opinion in question taken root, that although, during the past year, every dollar in gold which the Government could command would cancel from two to two and a half dollars of the public debt, not the slightest attempt has been made to command that coin, either by loans or taxes.

The table on page 169 shows the coin price at which the six per cent. twenty-year bonds were actually held in the market. Had specie payments been continued, bonds could always have been negotiated for at least this sum in specie, to the extent to which they actually were negotiated in notes. Probably they would have brought a much higher price, as the two great depressing causes which have diminished the value of all government securities would not have existed. These causes are:

1. The suspension of specie payments, thereby establishing the principle that if it were not convenient to pay a debt when due, payment might be indefinitely deferred; and the passage of the act declaring irredeemable paper money a legal tender for the entire principal of the public debt.

2. The depreciation of the currency, causing enormous profits to accrue from commercial and speculative ventures, thus discouraging investment in securities which only pay reasonable dividends.

The manner in which each of these causes has operated to diminish the market value of Government securities has been fully set forth in the fourth and fifth chapters. Allowing for their probable effect, our financial history as it would have been had specie payments been continued, and no notes issued, compared with what it has been, is shown in the following table:

WERE LEGAL TENDER NOTES NECESSARY? 169

		(1) Coin price of bonds, &c.	(2) Loss per cent. in negotiating.	(3) Buying power of gold.	(4) Amount of indebtedness.	Per cent. of gain by notes.	Per cent. of loss by notes.
1862.	1st Quarter	80	20	1.00	.80	20	
	2d "	90 *	10	1.00	.90	10	
	3d "	83	17	1.10	.91	9	
	4th "	78	22	1.15	.89	11	
1863.	1st "	71 †	29	1.20	.85	15	
	2d "	77	23	1.40	1.08		8
	3d "	82	18	1.35	1.10		10
	4th "	82 ‡	18	1.30	1.07		7
1864.	1st "	75	25	1.40	1.05		5
	2d "	70	30	1.80	1.26		26
	3d "	67	33	2.40	1.60		60
	4th "	70	30	2.40	1.68		68

Taking an average each three months, it shows:

1. The price at which bonds and certificates of indebtedness could have been negotiated for coin,

---

* At this time bonds were worth nearly par in coin, but this is because Government put none on the market, issuing legal tender notes to the public creditors. The brilliant victories in the spring of 1862 caused a great rise in the value of government securities.

† The public mind desponded, owing to the ill success of our arms during the past six months. Bonds in consequence very low.

‡ The victories of the past summer seem to presage the speedy fall of the rebellion. Lee is driven from Pennsylvania; Vicksburg, Chattanooga, and Port Hudson have fallen; and "the men of the West have hewn their way to the Gulf of Mexico with their swords." There is another rise in bonds, which, unfortunately, is only temporary.

or notes convertible into coin, as compared with the price in the notes actually used.

2. The nominal loss per cent. in the negotiation, to which the Government would have been obliged to submit in consequence of employing coin instead of notes. It is found by subtracting the preceding column from 100, which represents the price the bonds actually brought in paper.

3. The buying power of the gold, compared with that of paper generally, put lower than the price of gold, because there are many payments, such as salaries and old debts, for which paper has, up to the present time, been nearly as good as coin.

4. Multiplying the columns (1) and (3) we have the percentage of indebtedness *actually incurred* compared with what *would have been incurred* had specie payments been adhered to. It will be observed that up to the first quarter of 1863 there is a steady gain from the issue of notes; after that time a continual loss, which, however, does not become very serious until 1864. The loss is now increasing in a most alarming ratio.

Had a specie basis been maintained, we should probably have incurred an indebtedness of about $150,000,000 in each quarter. The gradually diminishing amount of coin which this amount of indebtedness would have secured us, would have been compensated by the increasing revenue from taxes, and the increasing cheapness of war material. The gain and loss in dollars from the use of legal tender notes may therefore be estimated as follows, for each quarter:

		Gain.	Loss.
1862.	1st Quarter 2d " 3d " 4th "	$30,000,000 15,000,000 14,000,000 16,000,000	
1863.	1st " 2d " 3d " 4th "	22,000,000	$12,000,000 15,000,000 10,000,000
1864.	1st " 2d " 3d " 4th "		8,000,000 39,000,000 90,000,000 102,000,000

Thus, according to the best judgment we can form, we saved $97,000,000 in indebtedness by the use of notes during the first year after their issue. This was saved because the notes, answering the purpose of money, were more acceptable than bonds would have been, and because we were enabled to pay off contracts made when gold was at par with notes after they had depreciated one-third.

But, since that time, up to the end of 1864, we have not only lost that $97,000,000, but $180,000,000 in addition. At the end of this period the loss is peculiarly great, because we are paying debt contracted when gold was at 260 with an *appreciated* currency.

In 1865 we shall probably incur an indebtedness $300,000,000 greater than we should had we adhered to the specie standard, though the war should end immediately, because we will have to pay debts in the appreciated currency.

Thus, owing to the unfortunate misconception of the true object of the notes, a misconception founded upon a total ignorance of the functions of money, and the laws which in practice regulate its value, a measure which might have been a limited source of good has been made to work us infinite mischief. The object of the notes was not to furnish the country with money to buy bonds with, but to obtain as large a loan as possible without interest. If the notes were not redeemable on demand, it was not only unnecessary, but highly mischievous, that they should have been universally receivable for loans.

The fact that our finances are in a far worse condition, and we, as a people, morally weaker than if we had never issued a government note, is of itself a sufficient answer to the question whether the notes were necessary.

II. *Was it necessary that the notes should not be redeemable in coin?* That it was desirable to provide means for redemption of the notes, no one will dispute. In no other safe way could they be kept from the depreciation and continual fluctuations in value, which experience has shown to be the universal lot of every system of irredeemable paper money, and which reason tells us must be its lot, so long as human nature remains as it is. In fact, redeeming the paper is the only practical mode of fixing its value. If, in the opinion of the Government, its obligation expressed by the note is as valuable as coin, then it will be willing to give coin in exchange for it. If it values the obligation at fifty cents on the dollar, fifty cents on the dollar it will give to be relieved from the obligation. At the present moment there are millions of dollars of notes, the holders of which would be glad to resign them to the Government at fifty cents on the dollar, but the Government will not give it! It is perfectly idle for Congress, or any other power, to enact, or proclaim, that a note has any definite value, while it is belieing its own words by its acts.

It was not *necessary*, however, that they should have been absolutely redeemable in coin on demand. We might have adopted Ricard's plan of redeeming them in *bullion*, instead of coin, or the less philosophical, but probably more advisable plan of redeeming them in a certain specified time, say sixty days after demand. Then, each holder of a note, on surrendering it to the Treasury, would have received a check payable in coin in sixty days. The money necessary to redeem the notes would have been raised by loans and taxation. When the Treasury was not pressed, it might have been advisable to receive checks which had already run over thirty days in payment of loans, and probably four-fifths of the checks would have been cancelled in this way.

All danger of panics would in this way have been avoided. Circulating money of some kind, to the amount of at least $200,000,000, the country must and *will* have. Suppose a panic-stricken public do rush to the Treasury with notes in such quantities that less than this amount was left in circulation; in a few days a great scarcity of currency will be felt. Notes will become as valuable as gold, and holders of coin checks will be glad to withdraw their demands for redemption, and exchange the checks back again for the note, to which, of course, the Government would have no objection. After going through this operation two or three times, every one will be careful not to present notes for redemption, unless he has more on hand than he will have occasion to pay out during the next sixty days. When every one does this, over $200,000,000 will be reserved in all, and this amount will finally be retained in circulation. Thus the evil will always correct itself.

III. Was it *necessary* that the notes should be a legal tender for the principal of the public debt? By the principal of the public debt we understand, not the sums owing to contractors, public officers, etc., for supplies or services rendered, but the bonds and Treasury notes issued by authority of Congress, in definite sums, under an expressed or implied pledge of faith that they should be paid at a certain time. These authorized acknowledgments of indebtedness may be divided into two classes: those already issued when the legal tender act was passed, and those to be issued thereafter.

To begin with the latter;—we have seen that what the Government really gives in exchange for the clothing, flour, shot, and shell needed for its armies is its bonds; that the legal tender notes are mere tickets entitling the holder to their equivalent in bonds, so that the transfers of notes, goods, and bonds may be made with the greatest advantage to all parties; that it is, therefore, the value of the bonds themselves we are to look after, rather than that of the tickets, or other money with which they are negotiated. It is now perfectly obvious that the value of the bonds must be less, how much less it is impossible to say, in consequence of being payable in notes. It is obvious than any person would prefer a bond, of which the principal was payable in coin, to one payable he knew not how, and would therefore be willing to give the Government more goods and more labor of every kind for it. Hence the measure in question must, in the long run, necessitate a larger public debt than if it had not been adopted.

In the case of the bonds already issued, the measure savors so strongly of a breach of faith; it so certainly involves all the evil consequences of a breach of faith, that it can be justified only on the plea of "absolute overwhelming necessity." Let us look a little at the necessity of the case. There are a great many things to be done in the world which seem very difficult when we look at them with our hands in our pockets, but prove quite feasible when we earnestly attempt them. When legal tender notes were authorized, the amount of the debt referred to, maturing in the course of the next three years, was as follows:

$7\frac{3}{10}$ Treasury Notes, ...	$140,000,000
Demand Notes, ...	40,000,000
Other Treasury Notes,* say . .	30,000,000
Total—about	$210,000,000

Let us recall a few items from previous chapters. Far the large portion of this debt was contracted by actually paying into the Treasury gold coin, or its absolute equivalent, at a time when nothing else would be received or recognized as money by the Government, and when no one supposed that any thing else would be so received or recognized. We have also seen that a national debt is due from the citizens to the Government, as fully as from the Government to the public creditor; that if every one

---

* The writer has no data, nor is he aware that any published data exist, for an exact statement of the amount of miscellaneous Treasury notes (mostly interest-bearing six per cents) outstanding at the time in question. But the actual amount cannot vary so far from that given as to affect the point he is seeking to establish, the feasibility of redeeming them by taxation.

contributed his exact share of the debt in the form of a tax, there would be no debt contracted; but as so heavy a tax would interfere with the business of many citizens, it is arranged that some shall voluntarily contribute more than their share, on condition of afterwards being reimbursed from those who have paid less. A debt is thus contracted. Paying the debt is nothing more than equalizing these contributions, so that every one shall have contributed his just share. The debt in question would have been paid off by a contribution averaging about three dollars and a half per annum from each inhabitant of the loyal States. To say that the Government could not pay off this debt in coin, is to say that it could neither compel nor persuade its citizens to fulfil their most sacred obligations; that it could not raise a tax of three and a half dollars per annum in coin from each inhabitant, and had not credit enough to borrow coin to this amount. A Government which can do none of these things, is at the same time bankrupt and *helplessly imbecile;* for if it were not bankrupt, it could raise the coin by loans, and if it were not helplessly imbecile, it it could raise it by taxation.

The plea of necessity is therefore at the same time a plea of bankruptcy, and a plea of helpless imbecility! No man who will hereafter raise it, is worthy to be a citizen of the Republic. And yet it has been urged by men not only professing to be patriotic citizens, but friends of our public credit.

IV. *Was it necessary or expedient that the notes should be a legal tender in payment of private debts?*

In a previous chapter we have described the great revolution in the views, feelings, honesty, and habits of the nation, and in the ownership of that property which is the result of laborious frugality, slowly and almost insensibly, but most certainly being produced by the operation of the legal tender act. This revolution, and the evils involved in it, were not unforeseen by the able men who framed the act. The statesmanlike speeches of Messrs. Fessenden, Collamer, and Cowan in the Senate against the legal tender clause demonstrate this, but the clause was nevertheless retained under the pressure of a supposed necessity.

The entire argument for this necessity is found in an extract from a paper of the Honorable Secretary of the Treasury read in the Senate during the debate. The respectable and responsible source from which this paper emanated, the weight which it carried in the legislative debates, and the enormous extent to which the legislation it gave rise to affected the ownership of property, alike demand for it the most serious and conscientious attention. The reasons referred to were quoted as follows:

"The making them a legal tender, however, might still be avoided if the willingness manifested by the people generally, by railroad companies, and by many or all banking institutions, to receive and pay them as money in all transactions, were absolutely or practically universal; but, unfortunately, there are many persons and some institutions which refuse to receive and pay them, and whose action tends not merely to the unnecessary depreciation of these notes, but to establish discriminations in business against those who in this matter give their cordial support to the Government, and in favor of those who do not make such discrimination. This, if possible, should be prevented; and a provision making notes a legal tender in a great measure prevents it by putting all citizens, in this respect, on the same level both of rights and duties."

This argument has a two-fold, it might be said an ambiguous application; and, in order to give it the accurate analysis proposed, it will have to be considered under two entirely distinct heads. When the Honorable Secretary says that many persons and institutions refuse to receive and pay the notes as money, he may mean either—1. That there are many creditors who would refuse to receive them for debts contracted before the passage of the act, and therefore with the understanding that they could legally demand coin in payment; or 2. That many would refuse to receive them as cash in payment of services rendered or goods sold on the spot; for example, that a drygoods merchant might refuse to receive them in exchange for goods, or a railroad company refuse to receive them in exchange for tickets. As the legal tender clause covered both these cases, we shall consider separately the two applications of the argument.

To begin with the first: the argument simply advocates all the evils which we have shown to flow from the legal tender clause. When this clause was under discussion *all debts* had been contracted by the creditor's delivering to the debtor moneys, goods, or valuable privileges, equivalent in value to a certain amount of gold coin; and the evidence of indebtedness given to the creditor was at the same time an acknowledgment from the debtor that the other was justly and rightfully entitled to this amount of gold coin, and a promise that he would deliver him either this amount of coin, or something else which he would be willing to accept as its equivalent. This amount of coin was as truly and rightfully the property of the creditor as if he had it in his own drawer; he is taxed for it as he would be in the latter case, and, if he owed a third person, that person could seize it equally whether it is in the form of a debt or in the actual possession of the first creditor. The argument of the Honorable Secretary, so far as it applies to the case under consideration, might be more fully and exactly expressed as follows:

Unfortunately there are many persons and some institutions who own coin which is in the possession of others, and who will refuse to accept these notes in lieu of the coin, and whose action thus tends to the unnecessary depreciation of the notes, &c.

So the legal tender clause was inserted, which compelled all these individuals to receive the notes in lieu of the coin, thus most unjustly depriving them of their just rights. Now the question arises, does this power of consummating injustice add any thing to the value of the notes? Not a particle! A little close thought (to say nothing of centuries of experience) will make this quite plain from whatever standpoint we view the question:

1. The absence of the legal tender clause would not, as we shall presently show, have diminished the circulation of the notes in the least. Nine debts out of every ten, and more likely ninety-nine out of every hundred, would still have been cancelled by a transfer of notes. The only difference would have been that, instead of paying notes to the nominal amount of the debt, they would have been paid to its real amount, that is, to such amount as the creditor was willing to receive and the debtor to give as the equivalent of coin. The debtor would thus be saved the trouble of buying the coin, and the creditor that of selling it.

2. It is perfectly obvious that the creditor would not set a higher value on the notes in consequence of having been compelled to receive them in lieu of coin, any more than he would set a higher value on the ashes left after the conflagration of his house than on any other ashes.

3. Although, from the position in which the debtor is placed, the notes are more valuable to him for being legal tender, this adds nothing to their market value. This will be made clear by an exam-

ple. A debtor owes $100. Gold is at 100 per cent. premium. If the notes are a legal tender, $100 of them will pay the debt; if not, he will be obliged to supply himself with $200 of them. The greater number of them thus required will rather tend to increase their value. To take a parallel example, suppose an inventor should contrive to rig a ship with half as much cordage as is now used. The ship owner would then find half a mile of rope to answer him as good an end as one mile would before, exactly as the debtor finds $100 in notes to answer him in place of $200 without the legal tender clause. But the manufacturer of the rope would not, on this account, be enabled to get a higher price for a mile of it.

4. The value of any article depends on the estimate set upon it by the community. Is there any single individual who will set a higher estimate on the notes because they possess this power of indefinite swindling?

The fact is, that the ideas which underlie the argument of the Honorable Secretary are precisely those which in the last century used to enact penal laws, or fulminate denunciatory proclamations against all who would not accept pieces of paper as the equivalent of gold. These laws enacted that persons who had goods for sale should sell them at the same rates for paper that they would have sold them for coin. The legal tender act does not go as far as this; it only enacts that those who had previously sold goods with the expectation of receiving coin, should be compelled to accept paper as the equivalent. But the argument would have applied with as much force to subsequent sales of goods. We might argue, for example:

"There are many persons and some institutions having goods for sale which refuse to receive and pay out these notes as the equivalent of coin, but charge twice as much for goods when paid in notes as when paid in coin; and whose action thus tends not only to the unnecessary depreciation of these notes, but to establish discriminations in business against those who charge no more for their goods than if they had been paid in coin."

Would not this argument be as sound and conclusive in favor of setting a universal tariff of prices as that actually used was in favor of the legal tender clause?

It will be remembered that all this criticism applies only to that interpretation of the argument cited, which presumes it to refer to debts already contracted. We still have the second application of the argument to consider, viz.: that if the notes were not a legal tender, "many persons and some institutions would refuse to receive and pay them as money" in current transactions, as in exchange for goods sold, or services rendered on the spot. It is fairly supposable that the Honorable Secretary had in his mind's eye a railroad company who would not receive the notes in exchange for tickets; a trader who would not receive them in exchange for goods, or a bank which would not receive and pay them as "bankable funds." At least, we may fairly take these as representative of the persons and institutions which would have refused to pay and receive them; so that if it can be made perfectly plain that no one of the above three parties would have seriously diminished the value of the notes by their action, then it may be considered as established that no other persons or institutions would have done so. But we must first look at one or two preliminary facts:

In the first place, the general acceptance of the notes as the medium of exchange of the country was inevitable. Paid by the Government to the army, the navy, and the public contractors, they would, through these media, have permeated every channel of business. National pride would have promoted this general acceptance.

Again, when the notes began to depreciate, they would have driven the bank money out of circulation, in consequence of the general fact that the less valuable money, *if accepted by the majority of the community at all*, always displaces that which is more valuable. In other words, the bank notes being redeemable in coin whenever the State authorities choose to force the banks to do so, would have been hoarded as gold was, while the government notes, not being thus redeemable, would have been kept for use as money.

The notes having thus become the "money" which every man would carry in his pocket to meet his current expenses, suppose that a trader should refuse to take any thing but gold in exchange for his goods. At the worst he would only put his customers to the trouble of buying the gold somewhere else; but more likely the customers would prefer to buy their goods where the money they already had in their possession would be received in exchange. Thus the trader would injure no one but himself by his actions.

The same remarks will apply to railroad companies. If they were determined to have their fares paid in gold, they had only to add the premium on gold to the currency price of their tickets, and then buy gold with the proceeds. This they can do just as well under the operation of the legal tender clause as if that clause did not exist. Finally, no bank could reasonably refuse to receive the notes from depositors, to be paid back in kind, nor refuse to loan them to customers on the same terms; the blow aimed at the value of the notes by such refusals would simply have recoiled on their own heads, by driving their customers to other institutions.

Thus reason agrees with experience in showing that it adds nothing to the value of a paper circulation to declare it a legal tender. Mr. Chase's argument is like a cloud on a mountain-top, which looks solid and impenetrable when viewed from a distance, but offers no more resistance than the air when we come to grapple with it. Every idea in it is a century behind the age. It belongs to the period when men thought that money was the great element of wealth and power; that it derived its value from the authority of the Government, and that all who would not set the government value upon it were offenders. Since men have cured themselves of the illusions of habit, and acquired natural and correct ideas of the functions of money; since they have learned that the interests of different classes of society are not antagonistic, but harmonious, and that the good of the State is the combined good of the citizens, they have seen that every one, whatever his religious or political opinions, will accept any kind of money at the same valuation and on the same terms that his neighbor will accept it from him, that no man ever accepts it on any other terms, and that forcing him to do so is simply robbery; in a word, that if a legal tender clause does not force paper money on an unwilling creditor it is useless, and if it does it legalizes robbery.

Paper money has been the curse of our country for nearly two centuries. Before the Revolution nearly every state had its "bills of credit" in circulation, the value of which was continually fluctuating. Sometimes they were founded on correct financial principles, as when, contemporaneously with their issue, a tax was levied sufficient to absorb them. Serious depreciation was then impossible; but commonly no means were provided for giving them any fixed value whatever, but they were left entirely to the mercy of chance. This long fit of paper money drunkenness came to an end with the Confederation. The cup was drained to the dregs.

When the fathers of our republic met to frame that Constitution which was to secure the blessings of liberty to their posterity, they had this century of paper money experience to look back upon. They saw innumerable evils, without any good to counterbalance them. Every argument for the alluring cause of the evil had been refuted by the bitter test of experience. They thought, and thought justly, that one of the greatest blessings they could bestow upon their posterity would be to protect them against this fruitful source of evil. Accordingly, it was enacted that "no State should issue bills of credit or make any thing but gold and silver coin a tender in payment of debts." To show the views of these prohibitions entertained by the next generation of statesmen and jurists, we quote the opinions of Story* and the writers of the Federalist:

"The history, indeed, of the various laws which were passed by the States in their colonial and independent character upon this subject, is startling at once to our morals, to our patriotism, and to our

---

* Commentaries on the Constitution of the United States. Chap. xxxiii.

sense of justice. Not only was paper money issued, and declared to be a tender in payment of debts, but laws of another character, well known under the appellation of tender laws, appraisement laws, instalment laws, and suspension laws, were from time to time enacted, which prostrated all private credit and all private morals. By some of these laws property of any sort, however worthless, either real or personal, might be tendered by the debtor in payment of his debts. Such grievances and oppressions, and others of a like nature, were the ordinary results of legislation during the revolutionary war, and the intermediate period down to the formation of the Constitution. They entailed the most enormous evils on the country, and introduced a system of fraud, chicanery, and profligacy, which destroyed all private confidence and all industry and enterprise."

"The prohibition to emit bills of credit cannot, perhaps, be more forcibly vindicated than by quoting the glowing language of the Federalist, a language justified by that of almost every contemporary writer, and attested in its truth by facts from which the mind involuntarily turns away at once with disgust and indignation. This prohibition, says the Federalist, must give pleasure to every citizen in proportion to his love of justice and his knowledge of the true springs of public prosperity. The loss which America has sustained since the peace from the pestilent effects of paper money on the necessary confidence between man and man, on the necessary confidence in the public councils, on the industry and morals of the people, and on the character of republican government, constitutes an enormous debt against the States chargeable with this unadvised measure which must long remain unsatisfied; or rather, an accumulation of guilt which can be expiated no otherwise than by a voluntary sacrifice on the altar of justice of the power which has been the instrument of it."

"It was the object of the prohibition to cut up the whole mischief by the roots, because it had been deeply felt throughout all the States, and had deeply affected the prosperity of all."

Such are the enlightened opinions of our wisest statesmen and jurists, and such the sad array of folly and wickedness on which those opinions were founded. And yet, here we are restating the sophisms, and reacting the history of a past century! The most powerful republic on the globe, with unlimited resources, adopting the last and most reckless expedient of a bankrupt Government, and men professing to be its friends declaring that this is its only resource! By what process have we brought ourselves into such a position? Our whole policy can be traced to two very simple logical fallacies:

The first fallacy was that *the main expenses of the war must be obtained by loans in some form.* We looked in the wrong direction for our money in the beginning, and we have most steadily and persistently looked in that direction ever since. When the President called on Congress for $300,000,000, instead of trying to devise some means of raising this sum by a direct tax, or at least inquiring whether a loan or a tax would be the better, it was universally taken for granted that loans were the only resource. As additional sums were wanted, we had recourse to more loans. When the Secretary of the Treasury called for —— million dollars, the idea of levying a direct tax of —— million dollars was never discussed, never broached, so far as we have any evidence never thought of. Finance committees simply racked their brains for devices to sell —— million bonds.

This course was productive of its legitimate and inevitable effect. Loans could be obtained on favorable terms only from that small class who were at the same time frugal, possessed of money, and possessed of confidence in the good faith and stability of the Government. As soon as this class was exhausted, the inevitable depreciation commenced. Government promises brought less and less in the market.

With the suspension of specie payments, gold " disappeared " from circulation. Alarmed at the increasing difficulty of negotiating bonds, the Secretary of the Treasury made an estimate of their future depreciation, on the supposition that they were negotiated for coin. He concluded that before $200,000,000 in coin could be obtained in this way, the bonds would fall to 50 cents on the dollar.

Here was an excellent opportunity for a change of policy. When government promises to pay would only bring fifty cents on the dollar, and when there was every prospect of an expenditure of eight or nine hundred millions a year, it was high time to inquire whether arms, ammunition, and clothing could not be obtained by some other means than giving promises to pay in exchange for them. Unfortunately, however, instead of doing this, it was thought that that credit which could not be obtained directly, might be obtained indirectly by some ingenious device of statesmanship, or some scheme of financial legerdemain. This was the second great mistake. The issue of legal tender notes, and of certificates of indebtedness, the issue of bonds and Treasury notes in a multitude of forms, the various devices to create a demand for government indebtedness, including that concentration of absurdities the National banking law, the gold laws, the prepayment of interest on the public debt, all these are mere temporary makeshifts in a grand attempt to achieve an impossibility. Had none of them ever been thought of, but had we kept on in the old-fashioned way of selling bonds exclusively for coin, our finances would have been in a far more favorable condition than they are. But we would still have been obliged to submit to large sacrifices, probably half as large as we actually have submitted to. The combined skill of all the financiers of the age could no more borrow $700,000,000 a year on favorable terms, with a tax of less than $200,000,000, than the combined skill of Alexander, Hannibal, and Napoleon could avail to win victories with an army which was to remain immovable.

The nature of this second mistake will appear more clearly, if we compare our policy with the reasons urged in favor of it. These reasons are found in the Report of the Honorable Secretary of the Treasury for December, 1862.

Mr. Chase here speaks of the suspension of payment of the demand notes as a "necessity." He says that it was "impossible for the Government to negotiate loans of coin except at ruinous loss," and that "a condition had been created by the suspension which rendered loans of coin impossible."

I have maintained that these statements are ill-founded; but let us admit that they were true in every particular. Why was it impossible to negotiate loans of coin? What was "the condition of things" which caused this impossibility? But one answer is possible: *The people would not trust the Government on any reasonable terms with the coin lying idle on their hands.* Grant Mr. Chase's premises, and there is no possible escape from this conclusion.

With such a statement of our public credit at

home, published to the country and the world in an official document, what gold value could we expect our bonds to bear? And yet Mr. Chase goes on to attribute a premium of 37 per cent. on gold, as compared with legal tender notes to "the ignorant fears of foreign investors in National and State bonds and other American securities, and the timid alarms of numerous nervous individuals in our own country." The premium is here attributed to its true *immediate* cause. But what caused these "ignorant fears and timid alarms"? Were they not to be expected when a complete financial system had been adopted, the fundamental idea of which, openly and officially vowed before the world, was that American citizens would not trust their Government with the universal money of nations on any terms but such as would involve the Government in speedy financial ruin?

That we should have initiated a policy founded on two such mistakes as those pointed out, is perhaps excusable under the circumstances. We suddenly found ourselves in a new and untried and most embarrassing position. There was not a man in the country who was qualified by experience to give us any advice, for the simple reason that there was not a man who had seen a nation suddenly attempt to raise money at the rate of $800,000,000 a year. The general principles of national finance were our only guide. These were almost wholly unstudied and unknown. It was, therefore, very natural that we should adopt, in the first place, the policy which nations in general have adopted of late years when called on for a sudden and temporary increase of national expenditures.

It was also natural, though less excusable, that when we found this path beset with difficulties, we should try whether they could not be removed, not reflecting that they necessarily inhered in the path marked out, and that every attempt to remove them was simply a waste of most valuable labor. In a word, that we should have adhered to a wrong policy was excusable when we had only the voice of reason (which was drowned in the din of war) and the teachings of history (which were forgotten in the turmoil) to warn us of our error.

But that we should have adhered to our error after it was made patent by our own experience, as well as by reason and the experience of others, is inexcusable. When gold attained a premium of one-third, the fallacy that the value of our bonds could be increased by an issue of notes, was perfectly plain. How was this premium on gold viewed by the financial authorities? Mr. Chase says:

"It is true that gold commands a premium in notes; in other words, that to purchase a given amount of gold a greater amount in notes is required. But it is also true that on the suspension of specie payments, and the substitution for coin of United States notes convertible into six per cent. specie bonds as the legal standard of value, gold became an article of merchandise, subject to the ordinary fluctuations of supply and demand, and to the extraordinary fluctuations of mere speculation."

Here the Honorable Secretary steers so close to the truth that it is wonderful how it escaped him. "*The legal tender notes are convertible into six per cent. bonds as the legal standard of value.*" Of course, then, the notes cannot be worth any more than the bonds, after enough are issued to supply the want of a circulating medium. Let, us then, discover what the bonds will be worth, and we can judge what the notes will be worth. The bonds, says Mr. Chase, will soon not bring sixty cents on the dollar in coin;—"loans of coin are impossible except at ruinous sacrifice." *Then the notes, also, must speedily fall to eighty, sixty, or even fifty per cent. as compared with gold, if his doctrine is true.* Or, the notes being the standard, gold must speedily bear a premium of thirty, sixty, and one hundred per cent.

Instead of accepting this inevitable conclusion from his own premises, Mr. Chase argues that the premium is greater than ought reasonably to have been expected. He makes the same transparent mistake that has been pointed out in the financial management of the French revolution, namely, that by issuing representatives of an article to circulate as money, he could permanently prevent the value both of the representative and the thing represented from depreciating. To prove that there had been no actual depreciation, he shows that there has been no general advance in the price of the most important articles of consumption. But this only proves either that those articles were unusually plenty, or that the equilibrium of prices was not restored.

No doubt he expressed the views of the country at large. Instead of accepting the rise in the price of gold, and of course the depreciation in currency and bonds as unavoidable facts, and endeavoring to frame some new policy, we began to carp at those facts, and attribute them to every cause except the true one, the unchangeable laws of value. To express my whole idea in a metaphor, we built our house on the sand, in defiance of the observed fact that all who had previously been guilty of this folly had their houses destroyed, and in defiance of the plain dictate of reason that a house so situated must be exposed to destruction. We can find excuses for this act. But when the rain fell and the wind blew, and we found our foundations being washed away, instead of seeking a better foundation, we denounced the storm, and attributed it to the machinations of our enemies. For this, enlightened posterity will never pardon us.

We have seen that the legal tender notes have been productive of a vast amount of evil which does not yet appear, while there is absolutely nothing to place to their credit. We have given one more illustration of the principle that high moral qualities aided by hard labor on the part of those who stay at home, as well as hard fighting on the part of those who take the field, is the only source of military power. Every argument in favor of paper money is a fallacy unworthy the nineteenth century.

There is but one way to set our credit on a firm basis, and we owe it to posterity to retrieve our faults by adopting this plan. It is to adopt a constitutional amendment to this effect:

Nothing shall be a legal tender in payment of debts exceeding $10 except gold coin, tendered in the amount of at least two hundred and thirty-one grains of pure gold to every $10 of indebtedness.

Enact thus, and the pledges of public and private faith will no longer be at the mercy of short-sighted politicians. Every man who loans gold to the Government will then be sure of getting his gold in return if the Government exists. The laborer who deposits in a savings bank will not find his earnings dwindle away when they ought to increase. The annuitant will know then that he is not to be defrauded out of a provision for his old age by any technical quibbles. Every one who holds a promise to pay money at a future period will know that the meaning of that promise is not staked on a die, but is as unchangeable as the Constitution itself.

This measure will not prevent the circulation of bank money or United States notes, whenever it is deemed advisable to issue them. It will simply protect the creditor in case the value of these notes falls below that of gold, by compelling the debtor to pay the real value of his debt, without reference to the value of notes.

Until this, or something equivalent, is done, public confidence can never be fully restored.

CHAPTER VIII.

THE NATIONAL BANKING SYSTEM.

The object of banks is to put into a different form that portion of the wealth of a community which is in the form of money. The circumstances under which a change of form is desirable, and the cause of the continual tendency to change, has been hinted at in treating of the financial elements of military strength. All that portion of the wealth of a community which is in the form of " Circulating Capital," is really lying idle. Circulating capital may be defined as all products of labor which are waiting to be put to their final use, or to reach their final destination. Thus, if a coat is one year in passing from the loom to the wearer, it has been in the form of circulating capital during that time, and the profits of the dealers through whose hands it has passed must include one year's interest on the price of the cloth. All coin circulating as money belongs to this class, because every holder is waiting to pass it off, so that it never reaches its final destination while in the form of coin. So does all the "stock in trade" of every merchant, manufacturer, or business man of any kind, because every single article is waiting for a purchaser. It is very clear that the profits of all these tradesmen must include the interest on their stock in trade.

If a method could be invented by which every article made should pass immediately to the final purchaser without waiting in anybody's hands, all this interest could be saved to the community, and wealth formerly invested in stock could be put into some other shape. This might be effected in two ways:

1. If the plan were such that it could be put into immediate operation by each individual tradesman or merchant, he could export his entire stock, and buy a share in a ship, or he could hire labor to build a foundry, or he could exchange for some article of luxury. The community at large would then reap the benefit, the tradesman would be as rich as ever, because he would have something to show in exchange for his stock, and the community at large would thereafter be enabled to buy goods cheaper by the amount which they formerly had to pay him as interest on his stock in trade.

2. The work of changing the form of the capital might be left entirely to corporations, who would gradually buy up the stock, and export it, constitute themselves the agent for the tradesmen, buy from the manufacturers and sell to the public at old prices, and thus gain the interest on the entire stock

while that stock was still in an entirely different form. The corporations alone would be benefited; but since no one would be injured, and since every one would be free to become a member of the corporation, this would give no ground of complaint.

This change of form is, however, almost entirely impracticable in the vast majority of cases, owing to the immense diversity in the quality of goods, and the total uncertainty respecting the demand for goods of any one quality. But, in the case of money, we have some $300,000,000 worth of circulating capital, all of precisely one kind and quality, and the demand for which is almost constant. It is lying idle, and yielding interest to no one. Whatever portion of this coin may be held by a neighbor of a bank, he can advantageously deposit there until he wants to pass it off. Then he can give his creditor an order or "check" on the bank for the coin. Perhaps this creditor also will leave the coin on deposit. Thus the bank will soon find almost all the money of the community lying idle in its vaults, although the ownership of it is continually changing. Thus we have a bank of deposit.

The bank finding all this coin constantly on hand can loan it out at the current rate of interest. Thus we have a bank of discount. The borrowers will probably still leave the coin on deposit, and as the applications for discount will be greatly in excess of the deposits, the bank may loan out many times as much coin as it has in its vaults.

9*

If the borrower or depositor wants to pay some one to whom a check will not be convenient or acceptable, the bank may give him in lieu of the coin a bill entitling the bearer to the coin whenever he demands it, which may be more convenient to him than the coin itself. Thus we have a bank of circulation.

So long as all the business of the country goes on as usual, the bank will be perfectly safe, though its specie reserve amount to but a small fraction of the debts payable on demand. But a panic comes, and every one rushes to the bank to put his debt into the form of coin. Then the weakness of the entire system becomes apparent. The bank owes debts many times exceeding not only the coin which lies in its vaults, but perhaps more than is possessed by the entire community. True, the bank holds notes from individuals exceeding its liabilities, but the latter are due *now*, while the former may not be due for weeks; and the debtors may be unable to pay them owing to the disarrangement of their business caused by the panic.

Against the disastrous effects of such a panic it is impossible to guard by any plan yet tried. If, indeed, the bank were required to keep coin enough continually on hand to meet all its liabilities, the danger would be entirely avoided; but this would defeat the very object of the bank. The coin might be idle in its vaults for a century. But, suppose the coin is loaned to the Government, to be repaid when the bank is in need of it? Alas! the critical moment when the bank will want it, will be just the moment when the Government cannot pay it, and when the government bonds cannot be sold except at enormous sacrifice.

A suspension under the circumstances seems like a necessity; and yet it is a moral wrong, for which we shall certainly suffer. The disastrous effects of paper money which we are now beginning to suffer, and are likely to suffer for a generation to come, are the consequences of the lax ideas of public probity which have been the result of bank suspensions.

The relative merits of the National and the State banks in their way of effecting these primary objects of banking, I shall not now stop to discuss. The difference between the merits of the worst and the best system that could be devised is but a drop in the bucket, compared with the interests affected directly by the making of notes a legal tender. All that our banks can do is to save the community some $20,000,000 per annum interest on capital that would otherwise be unemployed, and it is not likely that the best system will save $2,000,000 more than the worst; so that we may regard $2,000,000 a year as the extreme measure of the benefit which the community can gain by the introduction of the best possible system of banking. But we have seen that such a change in the value of legal tender notes as frequently takes place in a single week, may cause property to the amount of $50,-

000,000 or even $100,000,000 to be gained and lost. Considered simply as an improved system of currency and banking, then the new measure would scarcely have received attention alongside of interests so vastly greater. It was supported almost entirely on the ground of its beneficial influence on the government finances, and it is this influence which it is proposed to discuss in the present chapter.

The idea of loaning the capital of a bank to the Government is by no means a new one. When the Bank of England was first chartered, the entire capital was loaned the British Government. As the capital was increased from time to time it was immediately disposed of in the same way, sometimes at a very low rate of interest, and on some occasions even free of interest. If I am not mistaken, there has never been occasion for the return of the money thus borrowed, specie payments having been suspended, first by order in council and then by act of Parliament, at the only time when a necessity of the repayment seemed imminent. But the circumstances under which our National banking system was inaugurated, are so different from those of the British Government at the time referred to, that we shall only be deceived by any attempt to justify our action by the example of theirs.

Before proceeding with the examination proposed, there are two points to be firmly established respecting which great indefiniteness and confusion of ideas seem to prevail. There are, in fact, two great illusions which our policy has the effect to foster, and which it is to be hoped the country will speedily be rid of. They are: 1. That every one who takes notes to the Treasury, and exchanges them for bonds, lends to the Government; 2. That the National currency may not depreciate the legal tender notes as much as an additional issue of legal tender notes to the same amount.

The idea that any one who takes a legal tender note to the Treasury, and exchanges it for a bond, lends to the Government, is indeed a most extraordinary one. Nothing can more strongly illustrate the illusions of habit than the prevalence of this notion. The man who in the beginning of the war gave the Government gold, and the man who now gives the Government cannon, shot, and shell, receiving in exchange a note promising that the " United States will pay;" these are the men who loan to the Government. The debt is contracted when the cannon is received and the note issued, and the same debt cannot be contracted twice. The man who brings the note to exchange for a bond only changes the *form* of the debt, and that in a way greatly to the disadvantage of the Government, because the latter then has to pay interest equivalent to 10 or 15 per cent. on the market value of the debt. Clearly, the Government has no reason to be anxious for such an exchange, for it adds nothing either to its power or its credit. If the community prefer notes which bear no interest to interest-bearing bonds, it is to the advantage of all parties to let them have them in preference.

It may be replied to this that the notes were issued with the understanding that they were convertible into bonds at the pleasure of the holder, and derive a large part of their value from this privilege; that although the holder of the note may decline availing himself of the privilege for a day or a month, yet he would by no means be willing to resign it altogether, and the value of the notes would at once fall if he were deprived of it.

This is very true, and conclusively shows that the Government ought to effect the conversion when asked to do so, but furnishes no reason at all why it should wish to be asked. The notes are in fact redeemable in *bonds* instead of *coin*, and therefore the Government ought to effect the so-called redemption for the same reason that a bank, in ordinary times, redeems its notes in coin. That the bank shall be willing to do this is regarded as a matter of course, but if it should establish agencies throughout the country, offering inducements to holders of its notes to come and get them redeemed, the sanity of its directors would be seriously doubted.

Yet a disposition to convert notes into bonds does indicate a state of things favorable to the public credit. Let us see how:

Every legal tender note has two elements of value:

1. A money value, in virtue of which, as ex-

plained in the beginning of Chapter V., the sum total of the circulation must be worth from $200,000,000 to $300,000,000 *in gold*. If, then, the total circulation *of every kind* were kept down to $250,000,000, any serious depreciation would be impossible; because, if any general rise in prices should then take place, there would not be money enough to transact the business of the community on the increased scale of prices: the money market would become "tight;" there would be a general disposition to *borrow* or *sell*, with a corresponding inability to *lend* or to *buy;* and prices would then necessarily fall until the pressure was relieved and the equilibrium restored.

Dividing the total circulation by 250,000,000, we shall have the maximum price which gold can permanently command, supposing all the business of the country to go on as usual. The circulation must include *every thing used as money*, whether government notes, national bank notes, state bank notes, or hotel checks.

2. The legal tender notes have a value as a government debt, represented by that of the bonds into which they are convertible, or dependent on the hope that they will at some time be redeemed in coin. When their value as *debt* is less than that as *money*, there will be no conversion, the notes being worth more than the bonds into which they are convertible, because the latter cannot be used as money. Such is the very simple explanation of the state of

things in the winter of 1863, when a hundred dollar bond would only bring ninety-three dollars in legal tender notes, although the former bore 6 per cent. interest in coin, and the notes no interest at all.

When, from a rise in government credit, the debt value exceeds the money value, the notes will not all remain in circulation as money, but will be kept here and there by individuals for the purpose of being converted into bonds, or in hopes the Government will provide for their redemption.

Now, it is plain that, if the bonds were to remain as valuable as gold, the whole issue of the notes above $250,000,000 or perhaps $300,000,000, would come back to be exchanged for bonds as fast as issued. This rapidity of conversion, this continual demand for bonds, would indicate, but not cause, a state of things highly favorable to government credit, just as a high thermometer indicates a warm atmosphere, but does not cause it. It would not be the demand for bonds which caused them to be valuable, but their value would cause the demand. Now, if not satisfied with the natural demand for the bonds, we use artificial means to stimulate it, we act on the same principles with the attendant in a sick-room, who, being ordered to keep the thermometer at a certain height, effected the object by bringing the thermometer nearer and nearer the grate as the fire went out.

Thus, in whatever way we approach the matter, we arrive at the conclusion hinted at in the last chapter, that it is the gold value of the bonds in which our notes are to be redeemed to which attention should be directed; and that, when this is ascertained, the notes may be safely left to come in of themselves.

It can scarcely be necessary to go into a long argument to prove that the $300,000,000 of authorized national bank notes must depreciate the currency as much as the issue of an equal amount of legal tender notes. True, the National Bank money may be redeemed in legal tender notes, but this does not prevent them from competing with each other. Indeed, under our present policy, the law which provides for redemption provides for a mere farce. The paper in which the bills are to be redeemed will answer no end which the bill itself will not equally answer. If the bill were redeemable in gold, a holder might present a bill for redemption either because he wishes to keep the money and considers the coin more secure than the bill; because he wishes to take or send the gold to some place in which the bill will not pass; because he wishes to make payments to the Government; or because he intends to use the gold in manufactures. None of these reasons can be assigned for preferring a legal tender note to a National Bank bill. The latter are as secure as the former; they will be received at par in every place where legal tender notes will; they are received and paid out by the Government in the same way; and the "lawful money" in which they are redeemable cannot be made into jewelry. Thus the redeemableness of the national currency does not tend in the least to diminish the volume of it in circulation; and it is the actual volume of the entire mass of currency, and not the convertibility of one part of the mass into another, which determines the depreciation of the whole. If this were not so, the Government would have at command a very simple way of preventing the depreciation of its money. It would only be necessary to reduce the amount of outstanding legal tender notes to $250,000,000, and issue in place of the remainder demand notes not themselves legal tender, but redeemable in legal tender notes on demand. These notes would be precisely like the National Bank notes, except that they would be redeemable at the Treasury instead of the bank. They could be issued to any extent without serious danger of coming back for redemption; and if the National Bank notes do not depreciate the currency, neither would they.

We have had many complaints of the depreciation of the currency by the State Bank notes, but it does not seem to occur to the authors of these complaints that the National Bank notes are equally pernicious in their influence. The latter are even more pernicious, because, in making them payable to and from the Government, every thing that could be done was done to enable them to compete with the Government's own notes.

All parties agree that an increase of the currency

is an evil. When, then, a measure was proposed, the consummation of which would add $300,000,000 to an already expanded currency, we should naturally expect it to be looked on with suspicion. We should expect to find every one eagerly inquiring what benefit the Government would derive from the measure to compensate for so great an addition to an evil of already alarming magnitude. We should have expected the proposers of the measure, anticipating such inquiries, to have presented a careful examination of its effect on the volume of the currency, the resources of the Government, and the burden of the public debt. We should, in fact, have expected a balance-sheet, showing exactly what means would thus have been placed at the disposal of the Government, and the cost at which these means would be attained. If we examine the official documents of Congress with a view to find such an exposition from the friends of the measure, we shall be disappointed. Many of the reasons assigned had so little connection with the measures in question, that they might as well have been assigned as reasons for reënacting the fugitive slave law. Of reasons really bearing on the measure, and of sufficient cogency to merit consideration, only two were urged, and these two form the great foundation of its support. The first of them is, "That the people want a uniform currency which will be at par everywhere, and which will be receivable for public as well as private debts."

To answer this it is only necessary to refer to the notorious fact that the people then had, have now, and are likely to have for years to come, just such a currency in such inconvenient quantity that its value has fallen to one-half. From the very nature of the case greenbacks must be nominally at par everywhere, and of equal value everywhere, because they are a legal tender; and they are receivable for public as well as private debts. The enormous fluctuations in their real value are indeed a most crying evil, but the currency proposed is necessarily subject to the same evil as long as it exists, and indeed must exaggerate it. Thus the argument in question is like proposing to add more water to a stream which is inundating a city, in order that the inhabitants may have water to drink.

The great argument in favor of the measure was, that it would support the public credit and create a demand for government bonds. To this effect the Honorable Secretary of the Treasury writes:

"The Secretary has already mentioned the support to public credit which may be expected from the proposed associations. The importance of this point may excuse some additional observations.

"The organizations proposed, if sanctioned by Congress, would require within a very few years, for deposit as security for circulation, bonds of the United States to an amount not less than $250,000,000. It may well be expected, indeed, since the circulation by uniformity in credit and value and capacity of quick and cheap transportation will be likely to be used more extensively than any hitherto issued, that the demand for bonds will overpass the limit. * * A steady market for the bonds would thus be established, and the negotiation of them greatly facilitated."

To this it is sufficient to reply, that it depends altogether on the terms of demand whether it is beneficial to the seller of an article. It is quite possible for a tradesman to create a demand for his wares by offering them on terms so favorable to the purchaser that he is himself a loser by the demand. In the case of the Government we want to know not only that the Government sells the bonds, but also want to know what privileges it sells with them, and what it receives in exchange for bonds and privileges. What do the organizations give the Government for the bonds? Gold? No! Gunpowder? No! Any thing of use in carrying on the war? No! They give only the Government's own notes. They simply exchange a debt which does not bear interest for one which does. If they paid for the bonds in gold at par, there would be some foundation for the idea that the demand for the bonds was beneficial to the Government; under the actual circumstances there is none.

The Government grants the banks valuable privileges with the bonds; namely, the privilege of issuing notes to circulate as money. To appreciate the cost of this grant to the Government, we must revert to what we have just shown: that the sole advantage of an exchange of legal tender notes for bonds is found in the consequent diminution of the currency, thereby making room for the Government to issue the notes. But, when the exchange is made by a National Bank, the Government supplies the bank with circulating notes to the amount of nine-tenths the value of the bonds deposited, thus resigning nine-tenths of the sole advantage gained from the organization!

We may now proceed to a more exact examination of the effects of the National Banking system upon the volume of the currency and Government indebtedness. To give the best case possible to the supporters of the new system, we will admit that the legal tender notes are money, that the Government must raise $300,000,000 of this money to pay its creditors, and that national banking associations have this entire amount all ready to pay into the Treasury for bonds. To make the case stronger still, suppose that the Government has no alternative but the issue of $300,000,000 of legal tender notes, in addition to those already issued. Every one admits that this would be a very bad way of meeting the difficulty, so bad as to be totally unjustifiable, except in case of the most urgent necessity. Will it be best, I ask, to have recourse to the printing-press for the requisite notes, or to accept the offer of the National Banks? Let us see:

There are already in circulation, we will suppose,

$500,000,000 in legal tender notes. Only $250,000,000 being actually needed for money, the gold value of the notes, *as money*, will be fifty cents on the dollar. If the Government decides to obtain the $300,000,000 required for its expenses by the formation of banks, the process will be as follows: The banks pay the Government this amount of money, receiving in exchange therefor five per cent. bonds, interest payable in gold. At the same time the Government supplies the banks with "National currency" to the amount of $270,000,000 to circulate as money. After the Government has paid out the money obtained from the banks, we shall have the entire $500,000,000 of legal tender notes once more in circulation, and $270,000,000 of bank money in addition, making a total of $770,000,000. So the effects of the measure are summed up as follows:

The principal of the public debt is increased by $300,000,000, which has taken the form of bonds deposited with the Treasurer of the United States.

The annual interest is increased by $15,000,000 in gold, which, with gold at 200, would be equivalent to $30,000,000 in currency.

The currency having been increased to $770,000,000, its gold value as money remaining at $250,000,000, each dollar *as money* is worth thirty-three cents in gold; that is, it has fallen seventeen per cent. on its par value, and thirty-four per cent. on its real value.

To look at the other alternative: had the money been obtained by a new issue of notes, the effect would have been as follows:

The principal of the public debt would have been increased by $300,000,000, the same as in the other case; but this increase would have been in the form of notes bearing no interest.

The annual interest would not have been increased at all.

The total circulation would have been increased to $800,000,000 instead, of $770,000,000 as by the National Bank plan.

Thus, the only effect of the National Banking system is to increase the interest on the public debt by $15,000,000 *in coin*, in consideration of a diminution of the currency by $30,000,000; in a word, it is equivalent to borrowing $30,000,000 in currency at fifty per cent. interest, payable in coin! And this as compared with the confessedly very objectionable policy of an indefinite issue of legal tender notes!

How could such a measure ever be considered as beneficial to the public credit? Two reasons may be found for this view. One of them we have already referred to. *The measure was never critically examined on its own merits.* Legislators voted for it, because it was vaguely said to be the opinion of men qualified to judge, that the measure would benefit the public credit. It does not seem that any of the authorities in question, except the Honorable Secretary of the Treasury, were ever called upon to show, to the satisfaction of the Legislature, in what way this benefit would be attained.

Again, the financial authorities who supported the measure, forgot to take into account the great change of policy necessitated by the different circumstances in which the Government was placed on the suspension of specie payments, and the substitution of United States notes for specie. In fact, the reasons of the Honorable Secretary set forth in his first annual-report, made before the suspension of specie payments, were perfectly sound. He there depicted the evils of a circulation of government notes, and the advantages to the government credit of the proposed banking system. *Were the Government really going to refrain from an issue of notes, and were gold to remain the only lawful money, then the measure would have been highly advantageous to the Government.* Remembering that the two great operations of the system are as follows:

1. The bank loans its capital, in lawful money, to the Government;

2. The Government allows the bank to issue circulating notes amounting to nine-tenths of the capital thus loaned;

It will be understood that if this lawful money is gold coin, the bank actually makes a loan to the Government; whereas if the money is only the Government's own notes, no such loan is made.

Again, in the former case, the value of the coin received by the Government is not sensibly depreciated by the notes which the bank is allowed to circulate, because gold can be put to uses which the bank notes cannot; whereas if the Government receives nothing but paper, the value of this paper is depreciated at the very time of receiving it by the privilege granted the bank of circulating notes.

Had it not been for this oversight, we cannot but suppose that it would have occurred to the supporters of the measure, that it was designed to avoid certain evils, viz.: those flowing from a government currency; and that after all those evils had been accepted to their utmost extent as fixed and inevitable, the reasons in favor of the plan vanished.

If it has not been proved to the satisfaction of every unprejudiced reader that, under the peculiar circumstances in which we are now placed, the National Banking system is most deleterious to the financial interests of the Government, let us view it from other stand-points, and see how every complete examination of the financial operations involved in it leads to the same conclusion.

The law forbids banks from using their circulating notes to increase their capital. If the effects of the law are really beneficial, this interdiction is much to be regretted, because it prevents the Government from reaping those benefits as rapidly as it otherwise might. Let us see how rapidly the Government might otherwise raise money. A National

Bank is organized with a capital of, say, $100,000. This amount it pays into the Treasury for bonds, deposits the bonds with the Treasurer as required, and receives $90,000 of National currency, for the redemption of which in greenbacks it is responsible. This currency, when properly signed, is in every respect as valuable to the Government as legal tender notes, because it is payable by the Government in all cases where legal tender notes are. If, then, the bank could loan the Government these notes as an increase of capital, it would confer the same benefit that would be conferred by a new bank with $90,000 capital. The Government would then allow the bank to issue $81,000 of fresh notes, which the bank would again loan the Government. This process might be continued until the Government had received $900,000 from the bank, viz. : $100,000 in lawful money, and $800,000 in bank currency, which it can pay out to public creditors. Every thing will then be the same as if the bank had been originally chartered with a capital of $900,000. The notes will be equally secure, because bonds to the amount of $889,000 are deposited as security for their redemption. Then why is it that this operation was interdicted ? It is quite plain that in the case supposed the stockholders, by an actual expenditure of only $100,000, would draw interest in coin on $989,000 just as long as their notes remained in circulation ; that is, as long as they were redeemable in paper no more valuable than themselves. We may presume that it was not considered desirable to allow the banks to support the public credit in a way so highly advantageous to themselves.

Now, I ask, would this operation have benefited the Government, and supported the public credit? If it would not, neither would the formation of any number of National banks, for we have shown that the Government is benefited in the same way, and to the same degree, in either case. If it would, patriotism has been prevented from reaping a rich reward by the injudicious prohibition.

To view the system from yet another point: every National Bank note in circulation may be considered as representing a bond deposited with the Treasurer of the United States. The note is, *indirectly*, a Government debt: the bank owes the holder of the note; the Government owes the bank. The Government pays interest on the debt, not to the holder of the note, but to the bank. But the holder can present his note at the Treasury, and receive an interest-bearing Government bond in exchange therefor, although the Government is already paying interest on the debt represented by the note!

Can we not apply to this last operation the objections of the Honorable Secretary to receiving the notes of State banks in suspension in payment for loans? "Loans negotiated in this circulation," he says, "would be simply exchanges of the debts of the nation, bearing interest, and certain to be paid, for the debts of a multitude of corporations bearing no interest, and certain, in part, never to be paid." Of loans by the Government of National currency we may say with equal force, that they are exchanges of the debts of the nation bearing interest for the debts of corporations bearing no interest, whose only security is found in the guarantee of the Government itself.

The National banks are also supported on the ground that they are fiscal agents of the Government. Considering that their principal business as fiscal agents is to stimulate and facilitate the conversion of notes into bonds bearing fifteen per cent. interest on the value which the Government gets in exchange for them, it may well be doubted whether the Government can afford to pay $40,000,000 a year for their services. If they could make beef and clothing, shot and shell, for the army, they would be of some benefit as agents; as things actually are, they are of none.

The only banks which really negotiated a loan for the Government since the beginning of the war, were the old State banks. They secured the payment into the Treasury of about $141,000,000 in coin during the year 1861. Again, at the end of 1862, when the Government needed coin to pay the debt of 1842, the same banks came forward and loaned the gold at four per cent. interest. Since that time the Government has never attempted to borrow coin on any terms.

In conclusion, although the National banks are most excellent investments for the stockholders if every thing goes on smoothly, they are productive of nothing but mischief to the finances of the Government. But this mischief is of a different character from that of the legal tender notes. In issuing the latter we did indeed purchase a temporary relief, though at the expense of evils which will be felt for a generation to come. In the National Banking system we pay enormously for what is an unmitigated evil from the very beginning, with no benefit of any kind to counterbalance it. But this evil is not of the incurable character of the other. It will be practically removed whenever we make the banks pay the same price for the privilege of expanding the circulation which the Government is obliged to pay for contracting it.

THE END.

Any of these Books sent free by mail to any address on receipt of Price.

RECENT PUBLICATIONS

OF

D. APPLETON & CO.,

443 & 445 BROADWAY, NEW YORK

The Life and Correspondence of

THEODORE PARKER, Minister of the Twenty-eighth Congregational Society, Boston. By JOHN WEISS. With two Portraits on Steel, fac-simile of Handwriting, and nineteen Wood Engravings. 2 vols., 8vo. 1,008 page

"These volumes contain an account of Mr. Parker's childhood and self-education; of the development of his theological ideas; of his scholarly and philosophical pursuits; and of his relation to the Anti-Slavery cause, and to the epoch in America which preceded the civil war. His two visits to Europe are described in letters and extracts from his journal. An autobiographical fragment is introduced in relation to Mr. Parker's early life, and his letters of friendship on literary, speculative, and political topics are freely interspersed. The illustrations represent scenes connected with various periods of Mr. Parker's life, the houses he dwelt in, his country haunts, the meeting house, his library, and the Music Hall in which he preached."

Catechism of the Steam Engine,

In its various Applications to Mines, Mills, Steam Navigation, Railways, and Agriculture. With Practical Instructions for the Manufacture and Management of Engines of every Class. By JOHN BOURNE, C. E. New and Revised Edition. 1 vol., 12mo. Illustrated.

"In offering to the American public a reprint of a work on the Steam Engine so deservedly successful, and so long considered standard, the Publishers have not thought it necessary that it should be an exact copy of the English edition. There were some details in which they thought it could be improved and better adapted to the use of American Engineers. On this account the size of the page has been increased to a full 12mo. to admit of larger illustrations, which, in the English edition, are often on too small a scale, and some of the illustrations themselves have been supplied by others equally applicable, more recent, and to us more familiar examples. The first part of Chapter XI., devoted in the English edition to English portable and fixed agricultural engines, in this edition gives place entirely to illustrations from American practice, of steam engines as applied to different purposes, and of appliances and machines necessary to them. But with the exception of some of the illustrations and the description of them, and the correction of a few typographical errors, this edition is a faithful transcript of the latest English edition."

D. APPLETON & CO.'S PUBLICATIONS.

History of the Romans under the

Empire. By CHARLES MERIVALE, B. D., late Fellow of St. John's College. 7 vols., small 8vo. Handsomely printed on tinted paper

CONTENTS:

Vols. I. and II.—Comprising the History to the Fall of Julius Cæsar.
Vol. III.—To the Establishment of the Monarchy by Augustus.
Vols. IV. and V.—From Augustus to Claudius, B. C. 27 to A. D. 54.
Vol. VI.—From the Reign of Nero, A. D. 54, to the Fall of Jerusalem, A. D. 70.
Vol. VII.—From the Destruction of Jerusalem, A. D. 70, to the Death of M. Aurelius.

This valuable work terminates at the point where the narrative of Gibbon commences.

"When we enter on a more searching criticism of the two writers, it must be admitted that Merivale has as firm a grasp of his subject as Gibbon, and that his work is characterized by a greater freedom from prejudice, and a sounder philosophy.

"This history must always stand as a splendid monument of his learning, his candor, and his vigorous grasp of intellect. Though he is in some respects inferior to Macaulay and Grote, he must still be classed with them, as one of the second great triumvirate of English historians."—*North American Review*, April, 1863.

Practice in the Executive De-

partment of the Government, under the Pension, Bounty, and Prize Laws of the United States, with Forms and Instructions for Collecting Arrears of Pay, Bounty, and Prize Money, and for Obtaining Pensions. By ROBERT SEWELL, Counsellor at Law. 1 vol., 8vo. Sheep.

"I offer this little book with confidence to the profession, as certain to save lawyers, in one case, if they never have any more, more time and trouble than its cost. To the public generally, the book is offered as containing a large amount of useful information on a subject now, unfortunately, brought home to half the families in the land. To the officers and soldiers of the Army it will also be found a useful companion; and it is hoped that by it an amount of information of great value to the soldiers, and to their families at home, will be disseminated, and the prevailing ignorance respecting the subject treated of in a great degree removed."—*Extract from Preface.*

Hints to Riflemen.

By H. W. S. CLEVELAND. 1 vol., 12mo. Illustrated, with numerous Designs of Rifles and Rifle Practice. Cloth.

"I offer these hints as the contribution of an old sportsman, and if I succeed in any degree in exciting an interest in the subject, my end will be accomplished, even if the future investigations of those who are thus attracted should prove any of my opinions to be erroneous."—*Extract from Preface.*

D. APPLETON & CO.'S PUBLICATIONS.

Laws and Principles of Whist,

Stated and Explained, and its Practice Illustrated on an Original System, by means of hands played completely through. By CAVENDISH. From the fifth London edition. 1 vol., square 16mo. Gilt edge.

"An excellent and very clearly written treatise; the rules of the game thoroughly explained; its practice illustrated by means of hands played completely through, and much of the minutiæ and finesse of the game given that we have never seen in any other volume of the kind. Whist players will recognize it as an authority; and that it is a success is proved by its having already gone through five editions. It is got out very neatly, in blue and gold, by the publishers."—*Com. Bulletin.*

Roba di Roma.

By W. W. STORY. 2 vols., 12mo.

"Till Rome shall fall, the City of the Seven Hills will be inexhaustible as a subject of interest. 'Roba di Roma' contains the gatherings of an honest observer and a real artist. . . . It has permanent value to entitle it to a place of honor on the shelf which contains every lover of Italy's Rome-books."—*Athenæum.*

Heat considered as a Mode of

Motion. Being a Course of Twelve Lectures delivered at the Royal Institution of Great Britain. By JOHN TYNDALL, F.R.S. Author of "The Glaciers of the Alps." 1 vol., 12mo. With 101 illustrations.

"No one can read Dr. Tyndall's book without being impressed with the intensity of the author's conviction of the truth of the theory which it is his object to illustrate, or with the boldness with which he confronts the difficulties which he encounters. * * * * * * * Dr. Tyndall's is the first work in which the undulatory or mechanical theory of heat has been placed in a popular light; but we are sure that no one, however profound his knowledge upon the subject of which it treats, will rise from its perusal without a feeling that he has been both gratified and instructed in a high degree while reading its pages."—*London Reader.*

Life of Edward Livingston,

Mayor of the City of New York; Member of Congress; Senator of the United States; Secretary of State; Minister to France; Author of a System of Penal Law for Louisiana; Member of the Institute of France, etc. By CHARLES H. HUNT, with an Introduction by GEORGE BANCROFT. 1 vol., 8vo.

"One of the purest of statesmen and the most genial of men, was Edward Livingston, whose career is presented in this volume. * * * *
"The author of this volume has done the country a service. He has given us in a becoming form an appropriate memorial of one whom succeeding generations will be proud to name as an American jurist and statesman."—*Evangelist.*

D APPLETON & CO.'S PUBLICATIONS.

Round the Block.

An American Novel. With Illustrations. 1 vol., 12mo.

"The story is remarkably clever. It presents the most vivid and various pictures of men and manners in the great Metropolis. Unlike most novels that now appear, it has no 'mission,' the author being neither a politician nor a reformer, but a story teller, according to the old pattern, and a capital story he has produced, written in the happiest style, and full of wit and action. He evidently knows his ground, and moves over it with the foot of a master. It is a work that will be read and admired, unless all love for good novels has departed from us; and we know that such is not the case."—*Boston Traveler.*

The History of Civilization in

England. By HENRY THOMAS BUCKLE. 2 vols., 8vo.

"Whoever misses reading this book, will miss reading what is, in various respects, to the best of our judgment and experience, the most remarkable book of the day—one, indeed, that no thoughtful, inquiring mind would miss reading for a good deal. Let the reader be as averse as he may to the writer's philosophy, let him be as devoted to the obstructive as Mr. Buckle is to the progress party, let him be as orthodox in church creed as the other is heterodox, as dogmatic as his author is sceptical—let him, in short, find his prejudices shocked at every turn of the argument, and all his prepossessions whistled down the wind—still there is so much in this extraordinary volume to stimulate reflection, and excite to inquiry, and provoke to earnest investigation, perhaps (to this or that reader) on a track hitherto untrodden, and across the virgin soil of untilled fields, fresh woods, and pastures new—that we may fairly defy the most hostile spirit, the most mistrustful and least sympathetic, to read it through without being glad of having done so, or having begun it, or even glanced at almost any one of its pages, to pass it away unread."—*New Monthly (London) Magazine.*

Illustrations of Universal Prog-

ress. A Series of Essays. By HERBERT SPENCER, Author of "The Principles of Psychology;" "Social Statics;" "Education." 1 vol., 12mo.

"The readers who have made the acquaintance of Mr. Herbert Spencer through his work on Education, and are interested in his views upon a larger range of subjects, will welcome this new volume of 'Essays.' Passing by the more scientific and philosophical speculations, we may call attention to a group of articles upon moral and political subjects, which are very pertinent to the present condition of affairs."—*Tribune.*

Thirty Poems.

By WM. CULLEN BRYANT. 1 vol., 12mo.

"No English poet surpasses him in knowledge of nature, and but few are his equals. He is better than Cowper and Thomson in their special walks of poetry, and the equal of Wordsworth, that great high priest of nature."—*The World.*

D. APPLETON & CO.'S PUBLICATIONS.

An Introduction to Municipal

Law, designed for General Readers, and for Students in Colleges and High Schools. By JOHN NORTON POMEROY. 1 vol., 8vo, 544 pages.

"I have spent nearly four days in reading your book, and am willing to say, in reference to it, that, when considered in reference to its scope and the design had in view in entering upon is, it is a work of great merit. The topics are presented clearly, discussed with ability, and in the main satisfactory results arrived at. Parts I. and II., I think, may prove very useful to students at law and young lawyers, as there is a great deal in the history of the law, and especially in its sources, both common and civil, that is very clearly, briefly, and logically stated, and more available in the manner presented in your work than in any other that I am acquainted with."—*From* AMOS DEAN, *Esq., Albany Law School.*

Thackeray;

The Humorist and Man of Letters, the Story of his Life, with particulars of his early career never before made public. By THEODORE TAYLOR, Esq. Illustrated with a Portrait, one of the latest taken from life; View of Thackeray's House; Fac-simile of his Handwriting; Humorous Illustrations by George Cruikshank; and other Pictures and Sketches. One vol., 12mo.

"The author, Mr. T. Taylor, long resident in Paris, has been collecting information for many years, and has much to say of Mr. Thackeray's artist life in that city. The book is illustrated with a portrait and some curious original sketches."—*From the Guardian.*

The Iron Manufacture of Great

Britain. Theoretically and Practically considered: Including Descriptive Details of the Ores, Fuels, and Fluxes employed; the Preliminary Operation of Calcination; the Blast, Refining, and Puddling Furnaces; Engines and Machinery; and the Various Processes in Union, etc., etc. By W. TRURAN, C. E., formerly Engineer at the Dowlais Iron Works, under the late Sir John Guest, Bart. Second Edition, revised from the manuscripts of the late Mr. Truran, by J. ARTHUR PHILLIPS, Author of "A Manual of Metallurgy," "Records of Mining," etc., and WM. H. DORMAN. One vol., imperial 8vo. Containing 84 Plates.

D. APPLETON & CO.'S PUBLICATIONS

Principles of Political Economy.

With some of their Applications of Social Philosophy. By JOHN STUART MILL. 2 vols., 8vo. Printed on tinted paper.

"In the whole range of extant authorship on political economy, there is no writer except Adam Smith with whom John Stuart Mill can, without injustice, be compared. In originality, Adam Smith, as being the acknowledged father of the science, takes the precedence, as he does also in exuberance of apt illustration. But in rectitude of understanding, clearness and sagacity, Mill is fully his peer; in precision of method, range of topics, and adaptation to the present state of society, he is altogether his superior. The 'Wealth of Nations' now belongs, indeed, rather to the history of the science than to its exposition. But the 'Principles of Political Economy' is an orderly, symmetrical, and lucid exposition of the science in its present advanced state. In extent of information, breadth of treatment, pertinence of fresh illustration, and accommodation to the present wants of the statesman, the merchant, and the social philosopher, this work is unrivalled. It is written in a luminous and smooth, yet clear-cut style; and there is diffused over it a soft atmosphere of feeling, derived from the author's unaffected humanity and enlightened interest in the welfare of the masses."

The New American Cyclopædia.

Edited by GEORGE RIPLEY and CHARLES A. DANA. Now complete, in 16 vols., 8vo., double columns, 750 pages each.

The leading claims to public consideration which the *New American Cyclopædia* possesses may be thus briefly stated:

"1. It surpasses all other works in the fullness and ability of the articles relating to the United States.

"2. No other work contains so many reliable biographies of the leading men of this and other nations. In this respect it is far superior even to the more bulky Encyclopædia Britannica.

"3. The best minds in this country have been employed in enriching its pages with the latest data, and the most recent discoveries in every branch of manufactures, mechanics, and general science.

"4. It is a library in itself, where every topic is treated, and where information can be gleaned which will enable a student, if he is so disposed, to consult other authorities, thus affording him an invaluable key to knowledge.

"5. It is neatly printed, with readable type, on good paper, and contains a most copious index.

"6. It is the only work which gives anything approaching correct descriptions of cities and towns of America, or embraces reliable statistics showing the wonderful growth of all sections."

Queen Mab.

A New Novel. By JULIA KAVANAGH. 1 vol., 12mo.

"No English novelist of the present day ought to hold, we think, a higher rank in her own peculiar walk of literature than Miss Kavanagh. There is a freshness of originality about all her works, and an individual character stamped on each,—there is, moreover, a unity of thought and feeling, a harmony, so to speak, pervading each separate work, that plainly speaks original genius, while the womanly grace of her etchings of character, is a marvel of artistic excellence."—*Tablet.*

www.ingramcontent.com/pod-product-compliance
Lightning Source LLC
Chambersburg PA
CBHW022012220426
43663CB00007B/1057